W9-ACU-751

WORKABLE ETHICS

WORKABLE ETHICS

What You Need to Succeed in Business and Life

GERARD I. NIERENBERG

NIERENBERG & ZEIF PUBLISHERS
New York

Copyright © 1987 by Gerard I. Nierenberg

All rights reserved. No part of this publication may be re-
produced or transmitted in any form or by any means, elec-
tronic or mechanical, including photocopy, recording, or any
information storage and retrieval system now known or to
be invented, without permission in writing from the pub-
lisher, except by a reviewer who wishes to quote brief pas-
sages in connection with a review written for inclusion in a
magazine, newspaper, or broadcast.

Library of Congress Cataloging-in-Publication Data

Nierenberg, Gerard I.

   Workable ethics.

   1. Business ethics.   2. Conduct of life.   I. Title.
HF5387.N54   1987   174'.4   87-1680
ISBN 0-936305-02-9

Printed in the United States of America

Designed by Irving Perkins Associates

Published by Nierenberg & Zeif, New York

Distributed to the trade by Kampmann & Company,
New York

10 9 8 7 6 5 4 3 2 1

To Lily Nierenberg
and
David Nierenberg

Contents

I   *Workable Ethics Are Timely, Not Timeless*   11

II   *O Tempora! O Mores!*   17

III   *What Are We Searching For?*   23

IV   *Where People Are Today*   29

V   *Moral Use of the Scientific Method*   37

VI   *Ethical Maturity*   47

VII   *Kohlberg's Six Stages of Moral Reasoning*   55

VIII   *A Look Backwards—Thinking the Unthinkable*   69

IX   *Tests for Power, Morality and Time-Binding*   79

X   *A Tale of Two Bishops*   93

XI   *The Self-Made Man*   99

      Appendix A   107

      Appendix B   109

WORKABLE ETHICS

CHAPTER

I

Workable Ethics Are Timely, Not Timeless

THROUGHOUT THE AGES, cynicism has gone hand in hand with the public's perception of ethical standards. Despite the growing concern about business ethics, reflected in the demand for business school courses on the subject, the development of codes of industry conduct and the increase in government controls, the results have been appallingly meager. Morality as taught today bears more resemblance to etiquette than to rules for ethical behavior. Actions tend to be motivated by how they appear to others. As H. L. Mencken observed, "Conscience is the inner voice which warns us that someone may be looking." The business executive today is not so much concerned that someone may be looking, but that *everybody* is. And "everybody" seems to have a different set of ethical standards. This is what causes an executive to agree with Hamlet that "conscience does make cowards of us all."

Clearly timidity and after-the-fact justifications are not conducive to business success. Does this mean that immorality or, at best, amorality is? Certainly both have been and continue to be resorted to ad nauseam with no discernible lasting benefit to business or society. Even the "new morality" (based on absolute faith in the bottom line) began to lose its believers in the 1980's. Many American business leaders belatedly came to the conclusion that short-term success and immediate payoffs were inferior to long-term gains. Unfortunately, a majority saw the light only after their foreign competitors had begun to outdistance them.

With executives preoccupied by falling profit margins and the pressures of foreign competition, the search for rules of ethical behavior might seem as frivolous as for a condemned man to ask for a manicure. This is not the case. Nor is there an implication that ethics has no place in the modern world or, more specifically, the modern business world.

The celebrated Swiss psychologist Jean Piaget isolates the problem—What is the present position of ethics?—and points to a radical solution:

> The positions of ethics as a branch of philosophy may vary according to the moral philosopher, from a definite subordination to metaphysics, to an independence based on the study of moral experience. . . . The latter position is an extremely fruitful one and has this advantage, for anyone who believes that a progressive intersubjective agreement is the sole corrective which can serve as a check upon individual thought: it gives an analytical tool for all types of morality including metaphysical ones, while the converse is not true. *(Insights and Illusions of Philosophy)*

Many of those who, like Jean Piaget, study ethics today would evaluate morality based on their own experiences rather than use a strictly metaphysical approach.

This book will provide you with methods for discovering workable ethics that are consistent with scientific advancements and will allow you to discover where you are at present and how far you are capable of going. An observation by Albert Einstein in *Out of My Later Years* (1950) points the way: "Ethical axioms are found and tested not very differently from axioms of science. Truth is what stands the test of experience."

Alfred Korzybski, the founder of General Semantics, wisely suggests that creative morality should not be "approached from the point of view of any private doctrine or creed, but from a mathematical, an engineering, point of view, which is impersonal and passionless." He provides this signpost: "[It] must first be ascertained what Man is—what is his real nature and what are the basic laws of his nature. If we succeed in finding the laws of human nature, all the rest will be a comparatively easy task—the ethical, social, economic and political status of Man. . . ." Later he adds, "[When] it is clearly seen that man is a natural being, a part of nature literally, then it will be seen that the laws of human nature, the only possible rules for ethical conduct, are no more *super*natural and no more *man*-made than is the law of gravitation. . . ."* With these insights you will be able to make daily decisions that have lasting ethical consequences.

You will no longer be oppressed by "immutable" laws but will have at your command a workable process that is both "good" and good for you and your business.

In today's polarized world, every moral principle and every ethical value is under fire. Zealots of all persuasions stand ready to defend to the end their own parochial concepts of right and wrong. Understanding is out; fiats are in. Everyone loses; nobody wins. Whether we look for ethical truths in the prehistoric past or in yesterday's newspapers, the bottom line is that traditional ethics seems to do little or nothing to enhance the quality and productivity of modern business life.

One does not have to go far to discover a fatal flaw in traditional morality. The philosopher David Hume expresses it as well as any:

> The notion of morals implies some sentiment common to all mankind, which recommends the same object to general approbation, and makes every man, or most men, agree in the same opinion or decision concerning it.

---

*This and other quotations of Korzybski throughout this book are taken from *Manhood of Humanity* (New York, E. P. Dutton & Company, 1921).

Here is a closed and static world that does not exist and never has existed. Here there is no room for change, for creativity, for independent thought.

Alfred Korzybski places the blame:

If we go back over the history of civilization, we find that in all 'sciences', except the exact ones, private opinions and theories have shaped our beliefs, colored our mental processes and controlled our destinies. . . . Each of the disputatious systems has a large number of followers and each faction looks upon the others as deprived of truth, common sense and knowledge. All of them play with the words 'natural law' which they ignorantly presume to have the basis and content of their own particular doctrine.

The outcome is predictable. As Sir Henry Maine, an English jurist, remarks in *Ancient Law* (1861): "The time always comes at which moral principles originally adopted have been carried to all their legitimate conclusions, and then the system founded on them becomes rigid, unexpansive and liable to fall behind moral progress."

Korzybski's appraisal is even starker:

Philosophy, law and ethics, to be effective in a dynamic world must be made vital enough to keep pace with the progress of life and science. In recent civilization, ethics, because controlled by theology and law, which are static, could not duly influence the dynamic, revolutionary progress of technique and the steadily changing conditions of life; and so we witness a tremendous downfall of morals in politics and business. Life progresses faster than our ideas, and so medieval ideas, methods and judgments are constantly applied to the conditions and problems of modern life. . . . Medieval legalism and medieval morals—the basis of the old, social structure—being by their nature . . . opposed to change [are] becoming more and more unable to support the mighty social burden of the modern world. . . .

Today's business leader requires more than just a few haphazard rules for social behavior. What is needed is a thorough housecleaning. We must discard the idea that morals are immutable "truths" inherited from a long-ago past. Our modern-day advances in scientific knowledge suggest strongly that morals are not mere palliatives for pangs of conscience but are driving forces in shaping and improving the society and the world.

Business, in the vanguard of social progress and wealth, should recognize the enormous debt it owes to morals and should apply them creatively to contemporary business problems. Korzybski alludes to this debt when he refers to medieval morals standing in the way of progress. Jesus' metaphor "It is easier for a camel to go through the eye of a needle than for a rich man to enter into the Kingdom of God" was addressed to a young man seeking perfection, but in the Middle Ages it became a condemnation of wealth accumulated through commerce and industry. Specifically excluded from blame were the great nobles whose wealth was in land. Medieval churchmen taught that money was "barren"—incapable of producing wealth. Interest charges and usury were considered to be synonymous terms and prohibited by law. Not until 1545 was the charging of interest legally permitted in England. Other reforms conducive to the growth of commerce and industry followed soon after.

The great economic historian Richard Henry Tawney argues persuasively in *Religion and the Rise of Capitalism* (1926) that the Protestant ethic played a key role in the early growth of capitalism. In fact, perhaps to the surprise of cynics who thought it had all been exported to Japan, a recent poll showed that a majority of U.S. workers still believe in and try to pattern their lives on the Protestant ethic, now rechristened the "work ethic."

While this finding, if "true," would make the work of business executives easier, it is incidental to their present-day needs. We should recognize that ethics, like any other branch of knowledge, is not a static "given" but a living and growing process—one that we can study and profit from. If we can combine this newfound knowledge with a strength and excellence of moral purpose, we can afford to stop fighting over division of the meager spoils of the earth. Instead, we can utilize those qualities that are uniquely human to produce wealth sufficient for all.

How can this be accomplished? Korzybski provides an answer:

What I want to emphasize . . . is the need for a thorough-going revision of our ideas; and the revision must be made by engineering minds in order that our ideas may be made to match facts. If we are ill, we consult a physician or a surgeon, not a charlatan. We must learn that, when there is trouble with the producing power of the world, we have to consult an engineer, an expert on power. Politicians, diplomats, and lawyers do not understand the problem. What I am advocating is that we must learn to ask those who know how to produce things, instead of asking those whose profession is to fight for the division of things produced by nature or by other human beings.

This, of course, tosses the problem right back where it belongs— in the laps of business executives. They are uniquely equipped by experience and the need to excel to seek out the "right" experts and— equally important—to learn which questions are the "right" ones to ask. As a first step they would do well to accept Thoreau's challenge: "Aim above morality. Be not simply good; be good for something."

How can we respond to this challenge? First, let us answer this question: Can morality be self-advancing? Answer: It *must* be. If we are to consider human nature today and also deal with the momentous problems of today's world, a few rules for social behavior strictly derived from metaphysical speculation should be discarded along with other debris from the dead past.

CONCLUSION

Traditional moral rules are neither "good" nor "bad." In a process world, time and change have made them irrelevant.

Business morality should promote production and wealth for the benefit of all society. It should not promote "holy wars" over who should get the biggest share of a leftover piece of pie.

CHAPTER

II

O Tempora! O Mores!

KORZYBSKI WAS NOT THE FIRST nor is he likely to be the last to decry "a tremendous downfall of morals." The great Roman orator Cicero was carrying on the grand tradition when in 63 B.C. he declaimed: "Oh what times! Oh what standards *[O tempora! O Mores!]*!"

Two thousand years later, an article in the *New York Times* (September 13, 1983) contained this quotation:

> There is a ground swell in American medicine, this desire to encourage more ethical and humanistic concern in physicians. After the technological progress that medicine made in the 60's and 70's, this is a swing of the pendulum back to the fact that we are doctors, and we can do a lot better than we are doing now (John A. Benson, Jr., president of the American Board of Internal Medicine).

The article, by Bryce Nelson, makes a number of points critical of modern medical ethics, but they can usefully be applied to modern business practices in general. Here are some of them:

(17)

1. "Some experts" believe that medical schools can dehumanize or even brutalize their students who are overwhelmed physically and mentally by the demands placed upon them.

2. They see patients treated as nonentities just as they themselves are by the medical hierarchy. This tends to perpetuate the feeling that patients are mere ciphers.

3. Medical schools and certification boards are beginning to demand "high standards of humanistic behavior" in the professional lives of students and candidates for certification.

4. Altruism is not always the only consideration. As Nelson explained, "Doctors have come to realize that if they have established a good human relationship with their patients, they are less likely to be sued [for malpractice]."

5. Physicians themselves are sometimes the victims of callous medical care. One, who was losing his vision over a long period of time, was troubled that none of the specialists who treated him ever suggested existing devices and programs that might have had a palliative effect. He said, "I am troubled by the lack of regard, which is apparently quite general in the profession of ophthalmology, for the quality of life of the person who is visually impaired" (Dr. DeWitt Stetten, Jr., *New England Journal of Medicine*, 1981).

6. Refusals of treatment advised by doctors are "extremely common" and refusals are "generally based on factors within the physician-patient relationship, especially failures of communication and trust" (*Journal of the American Medical Association*, September 9, 1983).

7. Many physicians pay more attention to tests than to patients. Specialization, where patients are shunted from one expert to another, can fail to provide a true picture of the patient's overall health.

8. Some researchers have found that "dogmatism, negativism and cynicism increased" as students proceeded through medical school. It is probably not possible to teach compassion but role models in almost every part of medical education can help students to learn compassion and humanistic medicine.

No business executives worth their salt could fail to recognize that they share at least some of these moral dilemmas with their medical counterparts. Their recognition that there *is* a problem is probably at the same confusion level. Unfortunately, they both are likely to conform with H. L. Mencken's axiom: "For every problem there is a solution that is quick, easy and wrong." Take the "swing of the pendulum" metaphor that appeared in Nelson's article. This implies, like Cicero's anguished complaint, that olden times were better times and that we must look to the past for moral guidance. This simply does not work. Medicine, like business and commerce, has been so transformed by scientific and technological advances that what was familiar fifty years ago is utterly foreign today.

For example, one of the big features of the 1933 Chicago World's Fair, both literally and symbolically, was a large painting entitled "The Doctor." The bearded subject, frock-coated and chin in hand, sits through the night in a humble cottage at the bedside of a sick child. This prime example of Victorian bathos was proudly exhibited by the A.M.A. and attracted vast crowds.

Let us be frank. "The Doctor" was a cliché when it was painted, and was beginning to be recognized as one when it was exhibited in 1933. Today, the reaction of the general public to it would probably be derisive laughter. Why? Because this "role model" no longer bears any relation to the general perception of the modern-day physician, even one who has ethical and humanistic concerns. Who makes house calls anymore?

This is a major problem with much traditional morality. Instead of seeking creative change, many only want a revival of the past where things were simpler and "better." To say that this does not work is not to suggest that the great moral teachings of the past are irrelevant, only that they must be made relevant to modern needs. Nelson's article attempts to do this but ends on an uncertain note:

A good model for teaching compassion and professionalism can be an experienced doctor who is honest about his own fears. "Do you find it difficult to go into that room where the patient has AIDS?" Dr. Gorlin asked a young physician.

After the young physician replied that he did, Dr. Gorlin said, "I do too."

The two then went into the room to talk to their patient.

The article's ending brings to mind the biblical admonition: "If the trumpet give an uncertain sound, who shall prepare himself for the battle?" It implies that an admission by both doctors of being afraid somehow makes them morally superior. But what about the patient's fear? Physicians who are given the deference and respect of society owe the patient much more than a mutual admission of human weakness. What they regard as the end of a moral problem is only the beginning of a process that can lead to a moral good—the alleviation of the patient's fears.

Ethics today requires the full participation by all involved in the problem. That is, or should be, a major concern of every responsible executive. Along with "a tremendous downfall in morals" in our present-day society has been a precipitous decline of public regard for our traditional leaders in business and professional life.

The columnist Colman McCarthy gave an incredible example of the reason for this decline of public regard. Writing in the *Washington Post* (July 12, 1986), he told of an attempt by Jack Olender, a celebrated trial lawyer, to place an advertisement in the *New England Journal of Medicine*. Under the headline "Tragedy with Cat Scanner," it read:

> Important message to those who rely on CT scans: In Washington, D.C., a settlement of $3 million was obtained from a hospital that performed the CT scan and a subsequent hospital where neurosurgery was done. The 8800 G.E. CT Scanner was involved. The right and left sides of the film were reversed, and normal brain tissue from a 16-year-old girl was removed. Result: Permanent short-term memory loss. Answer: Inform other practitioners of this risk. Use a marker on the head rest showing left versus right. Make sure computer is programmed correctly—feet first. Use check list.

McCarthy continued:

> Olender's effort to place the ad was the follow-up of a pledge he made in late May to alert hospital staffs to heed the details. Olender was in a position to know. On May 21, he was the attorney for the family that won the $3 million settlement mentioned in the ad. In 1982, surgeons at Georgetown University Hospital operated on the wrong side

of the girl's brain, following the incorrect labeling of an X-ray by a technician at George Washington University Hospital. Cases have occurred in which surgeons have amputated a healthy limb or left instruments inside the sewn-up body. This time, a cut was performed for a tumor, but the wrong side of the brain was opened.

The patient, now 19, will need lifetime round-the-clock care. On the day of the settlement, the girl's father told a reporter that his brain-damaged daughter can learn nothing new and remembers things for only five to 30 minutes: "It placed my daughter in another world."

It also placed her in Jack Olender's world. At 50, he is one of the nation's premier trial lawyers. His specialty is the catastrophic injury case. If malpractice were baseball, Olender would be a starting pitcher in the annual all-star game. His record includes 18 cases with victories and settlements, each worth more than $1 million.

Olender is not little league. Nor is he another malpractice lawyer obsessed with attacking doctors and hospitals. "If I had 90 percent fewer malpractice cases coming in my door," he said last week in his Washington office, "I'd still have too much business to handle." His effort to place the ad in the *New England Journal of Medicine* was part of his own reconciliation program with doctors. He intended it as a comradely reaching out to the other side.

"I keep seeing the same mistakes over and over," he says. "With the medical technology that's available and with the learning that doctors have, people are being needlessly hurt by plain careless, dumb human error."

Here the story turns sour. Olender's ad was rejected by the *New England Journal of Medicine*. The $185 check was returned with a brief note saying that under the editorial discretion of the magazine, the ad "has not been accepted." When asked later by a reporter about the rejection, the advertising director declined to offer specifics.

Other medical magazines have also refused Olender's ad. *Medical Economics*, circulation 170,000, said it was a piece of "clinical instruction and we are not a clinical-instruction magazine."

As more rejections slips come in, Olender is having little trouble getting the message: "I was naive. I should have known better than to think that the medical industry would cooperate with me to help doctors help themselves and their patients. The medical journals are controlled by doctors. Doctors are so paranoid about malpractice that they reject any help from a plaintiff's lawyer, even when I wanted to pay for the ad to help them."

In our pluralistic world of business people and professionals, no matter how much the limits of authority are strained, no theoretical system of ethics can even begin to meet their needs. Small wonder that the *Wall Street Journal* in commenting on the increased interest in courses on "business ethics" suggested that the coupling of the two words might result in an oxymoron—a combination of contradictory or incongruous words. This may be so when business leaders are tailored to fit into a procrustean bed of traditional ethics. It loses all validity, however, when creative thinking is applied to the ethical problems business executives face. When they are given the insight and tools to make meaningful decisions, they come through. Most people want to do the "right" thing. Rarely would one intentionally choose the company of wrongdoers.

Can it be that we are forced to subscribe to William James's observation, "There can be no final truth in ethics any more than in physics, until the last man has had his experiences and said his last?"

CONCLUSION

If "olden times were better times," why did we change them? Quite simply, we didn't change them. They changed us, creating new needs to be satisfied and new rewards for business innovators.

Moral "laws" also must be adjusted and changed to make the system work. The satisfaction of needs is still a moral goal. Only the method has changed.

CHAPTER
III

What Are We Searching For?

WHEN WINSTON CHURCHILL WROTE AN EPITAPH for the great hero of the Middle Ages Richard the Lion-Heart, this was the curious result: "His life was one magnificent parade, which, when ended, left only an empty plain." A brief survey of Richard's reign might put this harsh judgment in its proper perspective:

In 1173, while duke of Aquitaine, he joined his two brothers in a revolt against his father, Henry II of England. Ten years later the same two brothers led a revolt against Richard in Aquitaine. In 1189, he again fought against his father, defeated him and became king when Henry died the same year. Soon afterwards he set out on the Third Crusade. Along his way to the Holy Land, he captured Messina and Cyprus, and married a princess of Navarre. With Philip II of France, he then stormed Acre, after which his buddy, Philip, returned to France to plot with Richard's brother John.

Richard remained in the Holy Land and tried to capture Jerusalem but failed. He did, however, conclude a treaty with Saladin that allowed Christians access to the holy places of Jerusalem. Then Richard set out for home. Alas, he ran into another buddy from the Crusade, Leopold V of Austria, who imprisoned him, then turned him over to Holy Roman Emperor Henry VI, who released him after Richard paid him a huge ransom (raised by his long-suffering English subjects) and surrendered his kingdom, receiving it back as a fief of the empire.

In 1194, he returned briefly to England to put down a revolt by brother John and to raise some cash for a new war in France, where mercifully he died.

If all of this sounds vaguely familiar, consider this excerpt from an article by Daniel Goleman (*New York Times*, August 24, 1986):

At 33, Bill O'Donnell Jr. had succeeded. He was vice president of Bally Manufacturing, had an annual salary of $150,000, owned two Mercedes Benz and an expensive house in Winnetka, Ill.

He also cheated on his wife, missed meetings he had called and used 4 grams of cocaine a day.

"I was pursuing the American Dream, and I thought cocaine would get me there faster," he said. "I was running through life so fast that I didn't see that my role as a husband and father to my three sons was disintegrating, that my business abilities were crumbling."

For Bill O'Donnell, cocaine proved to be one of the perils of the success he had strived for since childhood. But drug abuse is just one of many symptoms of a growing malaise: Not only Mr. O'Donnell, but tens of thousands of young people are finding that in achieving business success today, they have distorted their lives and fallen into emotional turmoil.

In the era of the 30-year-old multimillionaire, when success and money are more fashionable and sought after than they have been since the 1950's, the fast track is luring more and more college graduates with promises of power, prestige and big payoffs. But in these high-pressure, high-reward jobs—particularly those on Wall Street, in corporate law, the computer industry and in the world of the entrepreneur—psychotherapists say that many executives soon lose all sense of balance between their work and the other aspects of their lives. And that is an important loss: As Sigmund Freud said, the two hallmarks of a healthy maturity are the capacities to love and to work.

In the cases of Richard in the 12th century and O'Donnell in the 20th, the result was the same. Both left behind an empty plain—a pointless and unfulfilled life.

This prevailing sense of emptiness in the business world in the 1950's was what first drove me to study the negotiating process. It was not (and is not) a series of isolated steps (a high salary, two Mercedes Benz, a house in Winnetka), although each of them involves a degree of negotiating. Rather, it was a process that seriously affected past, present and future. As Alfred Korzybski said in 1921:

> The scientists, all of them, have their duties no doubt, but they do not fully use their education if they do not try to broaden their sense of responsibility toward all mankind instead of closing themselves up in a narrow specialization where they find their pleasure. Neither engineers nor other scientific men have any right to prefer their own personal peace to the happiness of mankind; their place and their duty are in the front line of struggling humanity, not in the unperturbed ranks of those who keep themselves aloof from life. If they are indifferent, or discouraged because they feel or think that they know that the situation is hopeless, it may be proved that undue pessimism is as dangerous a "religion" as any other blind creed.

Today, there is an urgent need to reexamine the fatuous question: What business does ethics have intruding on our working hours? Many feel that ethics is concerned with religious dogmas and accept or reject its role in business life on that basis. Others regard it as a sugarcoating for unpalatable "truths." To some degree, both of them are "right" and both are wrong.

Thomas Jefferson had another view, which he expressed in a letter to his nephew who was approaching manhood:

> Your reason is now mature enough to examine this subject [religion]. . . . Shake off all the fears and servile prejudices, under which weak minds are servilely couched. Fix reason firmly in her seat, and call to her tribunal every fact, every opinion. Question with boldness even the existence of God; because, if there be one he must more approve of the homage of reason, than that of blindfolded fear.
> Do not be frightened from this enquiry by any fear of its conse-

quences. If it ends in the belief that there is no God you will find incitements to virtue in the comfort and pleasantness you feel in its exercise, and the love of others which it will procure for you.

With this goal in mind, let us reexamine the concept of ethics in business and discover the process that will make you not only good but good for something.

Ethics and Time-Binding

In the 1920's Bertrand Russell wrote:

The hope of satisfaction to our more human desires, the hope of demonstrating that the world has this or that ethical characteristic, is not one which, so far as I can see, philosophy can do anything whatever to satisfy.

Although Russell was generally regarded as an unconventional philosopher and social reformer, in this case he joined many of his contemporaries in "denying that science or philosophy could provide a sound scientific foundation for leading the good life" ("On Time-Binding* and the Concept of Culture," 1952, by M. F. Ashley Montagu).

Montagu's paper celebrated the publication in 1921 of *Manhood of Humanity* by a then unknown author, Alfred Korzybski, whose views were "from 25 to 30 years too early. . . . [In] 1921 Korzybski was occupied with science and its relation to ethics, with science and its relation to values."

In the post–World War II years, scientists in general have agreed that they must take a more responsible view of their place in the world. Too many business people, on the other hand, have continued to ignore Korzybski's warning: "If those who know why and how

*The term "time-binding" will be described at length in later chapters (see index). Essentially it means giving equal weight to past, present and future in making ethical decisions.

[to further the happiness of humanity] neglect to act, those who do not know will act, and the world will continue to flounder."

How many business executives do you know who could cope with the following moral dilemma?

In 1986, a brilliant young scientist, Peter Hagelstein, sold his home and slipped away from his job at the Lawrence Livermore Laboratory where he worked on the so-called Star Wars program. A month later he emerged from hiding, announcing that he had accepted an untenured associate professorship at M.I.T.

Hagelstein had worked at Livermore for 11 years pursuing his dream of an X-ray laser that would take holographic images of living cells and molecules in the body and be a major advance in medical research. Instead, it was turned into a Frankenstein's monster. It inspired the idea of Star Wars, which was originally touted as an impregnable defense against incoming missiles. Instead, it also became apparent that it would be effective in knocking out satellites such as those carrying defensive systems. If it were to work, mutual deterrence would be replaced by nuclear superiority for the United States and would herald a new arms race. Hagelstein had innocently developed another deadly weapon that had no moral validity.

Korzybski saw quite clearly where the emphasis must be placed if mankind is to survive—namely, upon the understanding of man's nature and the development of human relations on the basis of that understanding: "Ethics is too fundamentally important a factor in civilization to depend upon a theological or a legal excuse; ethics must conform to the *natural* laws of human nature." He clearly stated the consequences of "a system of social and economic order built exclusively on selfishness, greed, 'survival of the fittest,' and ruthless competition," and prescribed the remedy: The period of the childhood of humanity was one of arbitrary thought and confusion. "The period of humanity's manhood will, I doubt not, be a scientific period—a period that will witness the gradual extension of scientific method to all the interests of mankind—a period in which man will discover the essential nature of man and establish, at length, the science and art of directing human energies and human capacities to the advancement of human weal in accordance with the laws of human nature."

CONCLUSION

Nathaniel Hawthorne wrote: "The greatest obstacle to being heroic is the doubt whether one may not be going to prove one's self a fool; the truest heroism is to resist the doubt, and the profoundest wisdom is to know when it ought to be resisted, and when to be obeyed."

CHAPTER

IV

Where People Are Today

IN HIS FIRST PUBLIC STATEMENT IN 21 YEARS, Nelson Mandela, the jailed leader of South Africa's black underground, rejected (on February 10, 1985) a conditional offer of freedom from the republic's president. To be released, all he had to do was renounce the use of violence. President Botha, however, saw no need to make a similar pledge.

Mandela demanded an unconditional release before he would negotiate with the Botha government: "Only free men can negotiate. Prisoners cannot enter into contracts." Paradoxically, by refusing to negotiate, Mandela *was* negotiating, but on a higher moral level. Instead of cooperating, he insisted on retaining his moral beliefs and leadership instead of exchanging them for physical freedom. Botha, playing his usual win/lose game, "lost" in the eyes of everyone except his amoral toadies at home and abroad.

The morals game as it is usually played all too often seeks to produce a "loser" for every "winner." Increasingly, however, people are realizing that at the finish there *are* no winners, only losers. Self-seeking men, desiring power rather than social benefit, claim morality as their exclusive possession. Members of the so-called Moral Majority, like their counterparts in South Africa, use God, flag and country to impose their will on "Lesser breeds without the Law."

A Lesson from the Past

Zygmunt Nagorski, vice president of the Aspen Institute, recalled the building of the Maginot Line in France prior to World War II in the *New York Times*, February 13, 1985:

> Consisting of heavy armor, the most modern fortifications, the latest and most impregnable antitank defenses, its purpose was to keep the German Army out. French soldiers in the meantime were left without a sense of purpose: they (and their welfare) were overshadowed by the line. Hardware rather than human life was elevated to the highest national priority—and it was hardly surprising, when Germans attacked and walked over the line, that the defending French Army simply melted away. . . .

Nagorski continued:

> Does history repeat itself? President Reagan's budget will in effect erect another Maginot Line. The President is sending a signal that the human component of America's defense comes after the hardware—and that the human component of the American social fabric is no longer considered to be of prime importance. How otherwise can one explain the deep and painful cuts in social spending that the President proposes? How otherwise can one interpret his disregard for those in our society who need the most?

In the same issue of the *Times*, the humorist Russell Baker offers this observation:

After 35 years of it, war preparation has become a habit—maybe even an addiction—that besides distorting the economy, imprisons the American mind. The men of Washington who deal with arms-limitation programs and high nuclear policy—one is always struck first with how brilliant they seem to be, and then by the resourcefulness with which their brilliance is applied to guarantee that there will be no limitation on weapons, no change in strategy.

Though often young men, they have the old man's devotion to serving the status quo. It is as though, having never known anything but the frightful uncertainty of war prevention, they were born old men and can envision nothing but an eternity of ever-improving killing machines.

The Russians, one assumes, are the same. Is it the Russians who have become like us, or we who have become like the Russians? You should choose your enemy carefully, the old saying goes, for that is the person you will end by becoming.

Since we have reverted to the old survival of the fittest doctrine in business and government, it is not surprising that there is a revival of interest in ethics and morals. But things are not working as they should. After-the-fact retrospection usually does not produce a moral human being, only a remorseful one. For example, early in 1985 the Mississippi House voted unanimously to repeal a law enacted before the Civil War. No longer, after more than 120 years, will it be lawful to kill a servant or a child when the fatal act is "committed by accident or misfortune in lawfully correcting them." The legislators, unmindful of any moral implication, did not retroactively specify whether the victims would now go to Heaven or the murderers to Hell. Only God knows for sure.

Hot Flashes at the Executive Level

During the summer of 1983, a federal judge in Omaha ordered a highway construction company to pay a unique penalty for fixing bids. Given a choice between a $2 million fine or a $325,000 fine plus five years' probation, the company chose the latter. There was a catch, however. The terms of the probation included donating $1,475,000 over a two-year period to endow a chair of ethics at the University of Nebraska. The judge ordered that the professor (salary about $80,000 a year) should be someone "of national standing" who would focus not only on business and professional ethics in general but also specifically on bidding ethics. The Justice Department appealed. It wanted a straight $2 million fine to be paid to the U.S. government but was turned down by the U.S. Court of Appeals for the circuit, which called the sentence "creative, innovative and imaginative."

A spokesman for the American Council on Education agreed that the sentence was "novel, unique" but expressed moral qualms: "On one hand, I don't want to look a gift horse in the mouth. On the other hand, there is something a little less than totally pleasant, proper. It seems a little off-key."

It would be difficult to disagree with that assessment. Even in this age of academic specialization, it is disturbing to think of a graduate student spending his time weighing the morality of an act that is a crime which might be—but rarely is—punished by a multimillion-dollar fine. After carefully considering the pros and cons, might the student decide (as many have) that the potential gain from bid-rigging far outweighs any possible penalty? Giving the defendant a choice of sentences in itself seemed to encourage that pattern of thinking.

If you were a rational bid-rigger, which would you prefer, a $2 million fine paid outright or a $325,000 fine paid outright and an endowment of $1,475,000 paid out over two years? Even though the judge said the endowment payments should be treated as a fine for tax purposes, it was still a pretty good deal.

What about the public? Did it get an equally good deal? Certainly the public benefit was greater than from another "novel, unique" sentence that was imposed a few weeks later. In that case a 70-year-old woman, listed among the 400 wealthiest individuals in the United States by Forbes magazine, was fined $5,000 and ordered to perform 200 hours of public service work. Her crime? As chairperson of the board of Hudson Oil Company she had ordered gasoline pumps rigged to cheat the company's customers. Neither the government nor the public benefited from that deal: Instead, they were harmed by it and both lost money on it. Compare it to a mugger who got a prison sentence for snatching a gold chain, and a singer-guitarist who got five years for possession of a quarter-gram of cocaine and a fire-arm. The mugger had only one victim, the owner of the chain, while the musician as far as we know only victimized himself. The two companies had many victims. But take comfort, optimists. Things seem to have progressed since the early part of the 19th century when Napoleon I observed: "Morality for the upper classes, the scaffold for the mob." We don't execute common criminals anymore. We send them to jail at enormous cost and try to forget about them. White-collar criminals are fined and sometimes inconvenienced and made to perform "good" deeds, such as compulsory public service work, to compensate for their public disservice.

As for that chair of ethics, will moving morality out of the court-room and into the classroom compensate society adequately for the losses it suffered from the bid-rigging? A recent assessment of what contemporary ethics can offer to business executives holds out little hope for practical benefits.

In "Ethics Without the Sermon" (*Harvard Business Review*, November–December, 1981, pp. 79–90), Laura L. Nash, an assistant pro-fessor of business administration at the Harvard Business School, has this to say: "Business has not yet developed a workable process by which corporate values can be articulated." One difficulty is that "corporate executives and philosophers approach problems in radi-cally different ways. . . . Like some Triassic reptile, the theoretical view of ethics lumbers along in the far past . . . while the reality of practical business concerns is constantly measuring a wide range of competing claims on time and resources against the unrelenting and objective marketplace."

To avoid "the utopian, and sometimes anticapitalistic, bias marking much of the work in applied business philosophy today," Nash poses 12 questions for examining the ethics of a business decision "that avoids the level of abstraction normally associated with formal moral reasoning."

1. Have you defined the problem accurately?
2. How would you define the problem if you stood on the other side of the fence?
3. How did this situation occur in the first place?

4. To whom and to what do you give your loyalty as a person and as a member of the corporation?

5. What is your intention in making this decision?

6. How does this intention compare with the probable results?

7. Whom could your decision or action injure?

8. Can you discuss the problem with the affected parties before you make your decision?

9. Are you confident that your position will be as valid over a long period of time as it seems now?

10. Could you disclose without qualm your decision or action to your boss, your CEO, the board of directors, your family, society as a whole?

11. What is the symbolic potential of your action if understood? If misunderstood?

12. Under what conditions would you allow exceptions to your stand?

After providing real-life examples to illustrate the uses of these questions, Nash concludes that "by avoiding theoretical inquiry and limiting the expectations of corporate goodness to a few rules for social behavior that are based on common sense, we can develop an ethic that is appropriate to the language, ideology, and institutional dynamics of business decision-making and consensus. This ethic can also offer managers a practical way of exploring those occasions when their corporate brains are getting warning flashes from their non-corporate brains."

These last sentences are troublesome. Perhaps in a homogeneous society like Japan's, a consensus might be reached on "a few rules for social behavior" that might possibly lead to the development of a business ethic. In a heterogeneous society like the United States, such a consensus is virtually impossible. One corporation's "common sense" might be regarded as sheer madness by another corporation in the same industry. Lewis Carroll, in *Alice's Adventures in Wonderland*, observes that "everything's got a moral, if only you can find it." For example, in the latter part of 1981 these two differing reports of statements were widely publicized:

The Business Roundtable issues this statement out of a strong conviction that the future of this nation depends upon the existence of strong and responsive business enterprises and that, in turn, the long-term viability of the business sector is linked to its responsibility to the society of which it is a part. (Opening paragraph of a statement on corporate responsibility)

"More than ever, managers of corporations are expected to serve the public interest as well as private profit." So begins the new pronouncement on corporate responsibility of the Business Roundtable. That this message was agreed to by the leading lobby for the country's largest corporations is important in and of itself. The question is just how, and how much, public service should be provided by the corporation. (Opening paragraph, "The Business Lobby's Wrong Business" by Paul W. MacAvoy, professor of economics at Yale University, *New York Times*, December 20, 1981)

If a distinguished professor cannot even quote the printed word accurately, where is the "common sense" that Nash hopes for? Here, words have been transformed to fit preconceived biases and forged into a weapon to smite the "enemy." It is not necessary to review every skirmish in this "holy war." MacAvoy clearly states the moral issue that he believes is involved:

. . . the Roundtable states that "the corporation must be profitable enough to provide stockholders a return that will encourage continuation of investment." In present-day competitive markets, profitable enough is all the profits that are available from production of goods and services. There is nothing left over with which to make the payments to these other hypothetical constituencies that the Roundtable elevates in its statement.

A similar attitude is held by another noted economist. "The Unsentimental Corporate Giver" by Lee Smith (*Fortune*, September 21, 1981, pp. 121–140) summarizes:

[A] different species of gadfly . . . opposes almost all corporate charity. Milton Friedman is supposedly the headmaster of the give-nothing school. "Corporations have no money to give to anyone," he insists. "It belongs to their workers, their employees, or their shareholders."

But he makes two big exceptions, which bring his philosophy pretty much in line with corporate charity as actually practiced.

First, he says, closely held corporations in which the managers are the owners may contribute directly to charity to lessen the tax bite. Friedman also approves of contributions to local institutions . . . when they provide "marginal returns to the company greater than their marginal costs."

A final quotation, this time from Andrew C. Sigler, chairman of the Business Roundtable Task Force on Corporate Responsibility, may serve to round out this discussion of ethical alternatives. It was written in response to MacAvoy's article:

. . . the character of stockholders has changed. At one time most of them were long-term, personally involved individual investors. Now large numbers of them are grouped in institutions as unidentified short-term buyers most interested in maximum near-term gain. Such interest must be balanced with a long-term perspective. The simple theory that management can get along by considering only the shareholder has been left behind in old economic dissertations.

Conclusion

We trivialize ethics when we reduce them to "a few simple rules." Nash reduces the universe to a random series of discrete episodes. Time-binding ties it all together with workable ethics.

CHAPTER
V

Moral Use of the Scientific Method

KORZYBSKI'S CONCERN about the "downfall of morals" was shared by many other thinkers in the first half of the 20th century. One of these was Jean Piaget, probably the most famous child psychologist of the century. A younger contemporary of Korzybski, Piaget began his higher education with the idea of becoming a philosopher. The reality of academic life soon changed his mind. In *Insights and Illusions of Philosophy* (New York: World Publishing Company, 1971), he states how "young philosophers, because they are made to specialize immediately on entering the university . . . believe they have immediate access to the highest regions of knowledge." In truth, he points out, they—and sometimes their teachers—did not have "the least experience of what it is to acquire and verify a specific piece of knowledge." His attitude was reinforced when in a social situation a Spaniard introduced himself as a professor of higher psychology.

"Why higher?" Piaget asked.

"Because it is not experimental," the professor said smugly.

Piaget observed that "Philosophers have long believed that they have the right to speak on every question without making use of methods of verification, and this is not a new phenomenon. But it is a much more serious matter if they take the results of their reflections as a form of knowledge, and even as a higher form."

Thus Piaget joined the "war" that had been raging among philosophers and scientists since the 17th century. The causes and issues of the "war" are too complex to go into here, but a major difficulty was that philosophers were suddenly forced to deal as best they could with newly emerging scientific thought. One camp sought to preserve the old metaphysic which subordinated the physical sciences to what Piaget termed "suprascientific knowledge." Their "enemies" changed over the centuries, but in the 20th century, both Piaget and Korzybski were champions of the concept that knowledge arises from (1) the gathering of data, (2) the formulation of hypotheses, and (3) the testing of hypotheses—in short, the scientific method.

All of this may seem rather remote from the effective use of moral principles by business executives, but it goes right to the core of the problem. No one today can afford to accept without question the perceived wisdom of the past, obtained by use of a priori reasoning— that is, reasoning from "self-evident" propositions. What seems self-evident to one school of philosophy is frequently regarded as abysmal ignorance by another.

When we attempt to derive our moral principles from the teachings of past philosophers we may end up with anachronistic ideas ranging from what Nash calls the Triassic Period (survival of the fittest, for example) to Korzybski's "medieval legalism and medieval morals." Worn-out moral principles are a hindrance, not a help, in today's business world. We should discard one definition of the word *perceive*—"to attain awareness or understanding of"—and adopt another—"to become aware of through the senses." Then we open up a whole new area of creative thinking. Rather than merely memorizing the outmoded do's and don't's of the past, we can construct, a posteriori (reasoning from observed facts), a set of moral principles that are relevant not only to the individual but to the business world at large. The systems that can be evolved are pragmatic, and with creative thinking are flexible enough to address general concerns as well as specific areas, such as establishing and profitably using moral principles in business life.

The Essential Third Step

Virtually everyone is quite capable of gathering data and formulating hypotheses. Their "error," to a follower of the scientific method, is most likely to come when they omit the third step—testing their hypotheses. No responsible business executive is likely to make that mistake when important elements like the bottom line are involved. The error is more prevalent when making value judgments, and these are essential elements in ethical decision making. Their hidden assumptions can short-circuit the process of testing hypotheses. Why should anyone bother with this third step when everyone knows, a priori, that certain hypotheses are unassailably true?

Consider these generally accepted opinions about juvenile delinquency in the United States and the measures society can take to remedy the problem:

1. Juvenile delinquency leads to adult crime.

2. Youthful offenders must be made to understand that if caught they will be punished.

3. Young people who don't work are more likely to get into trouble than "responsible and ambitious" teenagers who have jobs.

4. Juvenile delinquents must be expeditiously removed from the community in order to protect society.

If you blindly accept the above notions, you will get an argument from the U.S. Department of Justice. A 1982 report on juvenile delinquency, published by the department and based on a seven-year study directed by Lyle W. Shannon, disputes all four points. Shannon says: (1) "While there is some relationship between juvenile delinquency and adult criminality, the relationship is not sufficient to permit prediction from juvenile misbehavior of who will become adult criminals." (2) "Furthermore, to the extent that a relationship exists, it may be explained by the operation of the juvenile and adult justice systems as well as by continuities in the behavior of juveniles." (3) Youths who hold jobs are in fact more likely to get into trouble than those who don't. This position was confirmed again in a *Wall Street Journal* article, November 22, 1986: "After-school jobs may do teen-agers more harm than good, says Ellen Greenberger of the University of California and Laurence Steinberg of the University of Wisconsin. The sociologists say teen-agers holding part-time jobs do less well in school, have higher rates of delinquency, alcohol and drug abuse and are more likely than their unemployed classmates to develop cynical attitudes toward work." (4) Greenberger and Steinberg suggest that "the ultimate question is . . . how to integrate [delinquents] into the large social system so that their talents will be employed in socially constructive ways."

The report also makes the point that most youthful offenders who escaped detection had stopped their misbehavior by age 18 and only 8 percent of these said they had stopped because they feared getting caught.

As with many limited studies of social behavior (the data came only from Racine, Wisconsin), the conclusions reached have been subjected to attack from many sides, even by those who attempt to reconcile the report's conclusions with their own life experiences. For example, the columnist William Raspberry termed them "virtually unbelievable, flying in the face of experience, social science, and common sense."

Piaget would disagree with Raspberry whatever his personal experience. He would probably regard them as predictable and even understandable. While Raspberry might find it hard to believe that only eight percent of the juveniles were deterred by fear of punishment, Piaget might want to examine why even those few clung to a lower (chronological) stage of childhood development. He would understand the development in the other 92 percent in changing stages and points of view.

Moral Reasoning after Piaget

The American educator Vita Tauss, commenting in the *New York Times Magazine*, (September 18, 1983), presented a point of view that is consistent with Piaget's on childhood development:

> A mother who leads her child through a series of steps with the goal of learning to appreciate fine art is not nurturing creativity; she is merely manipulating her child. . . . The essence of creativity is originality. If parents want to develop creativity, they must have the patience as well as the imagination to recognize the *child's* discoveries.
>
> As far as beefing up science and math is concerned these are the tools which teach us how to approach our environment. By teaching the scientific method of approach to a problem and the mathematical means of collecting and processing data, children learn to appreciate the elegance and simplicity of universal constants and logical reasoning. From there, who knows what creative ideas can spring?

Lawrence Kohlberg, a developmental psychologist, has given additional momentum to Tauss's view. Taking Piaget's theories of growth and development, Kohlberg has applied them to the relatively new field of moral education, as opposed to the method of indoctrination. My book *The Art of Creative Thinking* (New York: Cornerstone Library, 1982) deals at length with Piaget's ideas and has this to say about them: "[They] have had wide influence far beyond the boundaries of formal education. One reason is that these ideas provide a classification of human development that can be applied to many diverse areas. They have an additional merit: although the various stages are necessarily arranged in a hierarchical order, no value judgment is necessarily intended. Each stage must be gone through chronologically and each is not only valuable but necessary for growth. The thing that differentiates a 'higher' from a 'lower' stage is that its principles have applicability over a broader range of human experience."

In an article on computer education in public schools, Ruth Cossey of the University of California's Lawrence Hall of Science was quoted as drawing this distinction between computer use in richer and poorer neighborhood schools: "One group [the rich] tells [gives orders to] the computer what to do; the other sees it as a taskmaster. The group that has that power to tell will get ahead."

Kohlberg divides the development of moral reasoning into three levels and six stages. The stages can be seen as opportunities of where we can go, not where we have stopped.

Preconventional Morality

STAGE ONE: The individual's chief concern is to avoid punishment by pleasing (or at least not annoying or angering) a parental or other authority figure. Good and bad are not rational choices but only what the authority figure says they are.

STAGE TWO: Actions are no longer considered "good" or "bad" in an absolute sense. Punishment is still a factor, but the threat of it does not lead to blind conformity. Now the name of the game is: "Maximize pleasure. Minimize pain." "You scratch my back and I'll scratch yours" and "What's in it for me?" are operant. There is an awareness of other people and their needs, but both are to be manipulated to one's own advantage.

Conventional Morality

STAGE THREE: This stage marks the beginning of a radical shift outward from the egocentric child of preconventional morality to one aware of the society he or she lives in. There is a rather Pavlovian response to praise ("Good boy"), or blame ("Bad girl"), but instead of being ruled by blind fear (stage one) or selfish pleasure (stage two), the child strives to help and please members of the group(s) to which he or she belongs. The group instills its moral principles in the child through its approval or disapproval. Belonging, not being an outcast, becomes a powerful incentive to conform to the group's expectations.

STAGE FOUR:

Benjamin Franklin, while signing the Declaration of Independence, summed up stage four moral considerations nicely: "We must all hang together, else we shall all hang separately." The individual recognizes that his own rights and those of his group or faction must be balanced by society's need for law and order. In times of grave peril to the state, it is the moral duty of individuals and groups to subordinate their needs to those of the state. Personal relationships change, becoming more rational, objective and realistic in contrast to stage three's subjectivity and sentimentality. They are based less on fear of disapproval than on an ardent desire to advance the interests of the state or, rather, what is perceived to be those interests.

Postconventional Morality

STAGE FIVE:

Unlike stage four, where the law is sacred and must always be obeyed, the stage five moralist seeks consensus in a pluralistic society. Rigid standards and strict obedience of the rules are less important than reaching a compromise among conflicting groups. The result is never wholly satisfactory to any of the factions but it is "the best that can be done under the circumstances." The law of the land is no longer necessarily paramount. For example, the Nuremberg trials after World War II depended on a stage five concept that a "law of mankind" took precedence over the laws of a (defeated) nation. Actions that were "perfectly legal" in World War II Germany became hanging offenses when viewed by stage five moralists on the victorious Allied side.

STAGE SIX:

What is paramount is that you alone have chosen the principles by which you live and are ready to act alone if need be to fulfill what you believe in. This is the culmination of Kohlberg's stages of development of a fully mature and autonomous moral human being. Moral principles chosen by a parent, an egocentric self, or a group or a society as a whole are irrelevant at stage six—except insofar as they can shed light on the motivations of other human beings. Compromises among competing moral principles are equally irrelevant to the stage six moralist.

"This above all," wrote Shakespeare, "to thine own self be true, and it must follow, as the night the day, thou canst not then be false to any man." The statement adequately sums up Kohlberg's sixth stage of moral development.

Finally, consider this quotation again: "One group tells the computer what to do; the other sees it as a taskmaster." The first five stages of traditional morality put you in a subservient role. They become your moral taskmaster. The sixth stage can give you the power to achieve what *you* want through workable ethics.

CONCLUSION

Hypotheses that have not been tested should have no place in making an ethical decision any more than they should in making business decisions. The risk of losing is too great in both cases.

If you are driven by ethical "laws," you become their slave. If you use them as milestones to assess your progress on the way to moral maturity, you may achieve some "good" for yourself and for society.

There is no "final solution" in our search for moral truth. Goethe, after a long and rich creative life, demanded on his deathbed: "More light."

CHAPTER
VI

Ethical Maturity

ETHICS IS THE STUDY and evaluation of human conduct according to a set of moral principles and values. After that has been said, consensus vanishes and confusion reigns. You may choose to custom-tailor a set of moral principles that is uniquely your own, or you may accept the duties and obligations that a group imposes upon you. You may join any number of schools of moral philosophy, such as empiricism, rationalism, intuitionism or hedonism. For many adults, however, ethics consists of a conglomeration of contradictory, often misquoted and frequently misunderstood rules of conduct as taught by moral philosophers of the ancient or recent past. Their practical application to a particular person in a specific time and place is tenuous at best. We all have memorized statements that express humanity's noblest aspirations but we have also been bemused by moral admonitions that have lost their relevance—if indeed they ever had any. Example: The 6th century B.C. Greek philosopher Pythagoras is reported to have taught: "Abstain from beans."

Bergen Evans in the *Dictionary of Quotations* (New York: Delacorte Press, 1978) comments on this famous maxim: "What is interesting is the variety of interpretations that, through the ages, has been placed on this admonition. Some say it means just what it says and adduce many hurtful qualities of beans. Others say it is a parable and means 'Be chaste!' Still others say it means 'Stay out of politics!' " A sage would not have to strain the limits of credulity to make the system work nearly as much as these moral teachers confronted with and confounded by a bean. They bring to mind the biblical metaphor: "Blind guides, which strain at a gnat and swallow a camel."

Business executives often experience a similar confusion when they try to reconcile modern scientific knowledge with traditional morality. Instead of the familiar world they deal with every day, they are confronted by a closed system that only grudgingly yields to change. The narrow art of casuistry—applying general moral laws to resolve or rationalize problems in particular cases—provides the only opportunity to apply a modicum of creativity to these moral considerations. At best, this may produce "a few rules for social behavior that are based on common sense." At worst, it will serve as a reminder that casuistry has a second meaning—specious argument.

Since we are all different, living different lives, our moral development varies. Thus far we have dealt with Kohlberg's stages of moral development as predictable steps an individual *may* take during the process of maturing. No value judgment is intended or implied in assigning a particular stage in Kohlberg's system to a human action. A stage two action is no better or worse than a stage six action *if that is all a person is capable of*. If it is not, then a self-imposed limitation has prevented that person from realizing his or her full potential.

Instead of regarding Kohlberg's system as a ladder leading upward, it may be seen as a series of concentric circles, each one encompassing a more expansive moral attitude until eventually all of humanity is included. This view of moral development serves our purpose much better than the traditional idealistic goal of moral "superiority." Today's business executive is much less likely to aspire to sainthood than to self-realization. Some would even settle for William Congreve's wish: "Would she could make of me a saint, or I of her a sinner."

Returning to the boardroom from a 17th-century bedroom, let's examine how this new perspective on broadening Kohlberg's system can assist us in making better business decisions, how we can "do business" with practically anyone without "selling our soul" or losing our shirt.

A Gender Gap?

As with many theories advanced by social scientists, Kohlberg's moral stages cannot be "proved" by the scientific method's exacting standards. There are, of course, a number of dissenters who attack the theory for a variety of reasons. Prominent among these is Carol Gilligan, a professor at the Harvard School of Education and an outspoken feminist. Her book *In a Different Voice* (Cambridge: Harvard University Press, 1982) attracted widespread attention after she joined with President Reagan's pollster during the 1982 election to expound on the newly discovered "gender gap." Central to her book is the argument that psychologists from Freud to Piaget have depended almost exclusively on observations of boys and men in establishing their developmental theories. The result has been, according to this view, Freud's famous outburst: "The great question . . . which I have not been able to answer, despite my thirty years of research into the feminine soul, is 'What does a woman want?' "

Whatever one may think of Gilligan's ideas, her radically different point of view provides creative insights into the structure, order and relation of age-old moral dilemmas. Two quotations from the book may stimulate your thoughts on moral reasoning:

> The moral imperative that emerges repeatedly in interviews with women is an injunction to care, a responsibility to discern and alleviate the "real and recognizable trouble" of this world. For men, the moral imperative appears rather as an injunction to respect the rights of others and thus to protect from interference the rights to life and self-fulfillment.

> Girls, Piaget observes, have a more "pragmatic" attitude toward rules, "regarding a rule as good as long as the game repaid it." Girls were

more tolerant in their attitudes toward rules, more willing to make exceptions, and more easily reconciled to innovations. As a result, the legal sense, which Piaget considers essential to moral development, "is far less developed in little girls than in boys."

The bias that leads Piaget to equate male development with child development also colors [Janet] Lever's work. The assumption that shapes her discussion of results is that the male model is the better one since it fits the requirements for modern corporate success. In contrast, the sensitivity and care for the feelings of others that girls develop through their play have little market value and can impede professional success.

The quotations provide an insight into the opposing, mutually exclusive views that seem to exist in any theory of moral development. Gilligan seems to imply that Kohlberg's stages one through four apply to boys and stages one through five to girls. Certainly such a theory might help to explain some of the characteristics of the transition that seems to occur when a person attempts to go from stage four to five.

Meg Greenfield, the editor and columnist, dealt with the characteristics of this transition point in *The Washington Post* column (November 24, 1982) on the Roman Catholic bishops and their proposed pastoral letter on nuclear warfare:

In our pop culture over the years we have habitually confused virtue and a concern with moral values with denatured, unworldly, sissy figures—cutesy Barry Fitzgerald priests, or the stock war-time chaplain who, after a namby-pamby irrelevant existence up to the last reel, finally gets sore . . . steps up to man an ack-ack gun . . . to the overwhelming applause of the audience.

Here one encounters the maniacal compartmentalization of our modern life, the hubris of the politicians and bureaucrats and "experts" with their terrible notion that all is process and technique, devoid of any need of a human or spiritual dimension.

Korzybski has pointed out that there is an enormous disparity between progress in the exact sciences, where knowledge has increased by geometrical progression, and the social sciences, which have developed much more slowly by simple arithmetic progression. Thus we have moralists and lawyers quibbling over the origin of laws that are no longer relevant to present-day reality. Even Kohlberg's speculations about moral development present a plausible explanation of where we have been, but once we have arrived at stage six we realize we have reached the top and there is no place else to go.

Philip Geyelin (*Washington Post*, November 26, 1982), in talking about the professional football players' strike, might as well be describing the difficulties that accompany our moral development to stage six: Ed Garvey, the players' negotiator, "contrived to frustrate his followers, alienate fans, stiffen management and wind up with a settlement materially less valuable than the club-owners' original offer. Leaving aside the rights and wrongs, it was a triumph for futility, unfulfilled goals and misplaced self-interest."

Our problems will not suddenly evaporate when we have reached "moral maturity." Moral laws, after all, embody structures, orders and relations that were relevant in the past. To advance swiftly and successfully into the vastly more complex present we need new guides to help us make morality a living creative force. A good place to start is with metamotivation, a concept of the psychologist A. H. Maslow, which he describes as the biological rooting of the value-life. Instead of using the limited social sciences approach to formulate a few simple rules of morality, we can begin to harness the latent power of other scientific methods. Instead of metaphysical speculation, we begin to grasp a workable ethics.

Metamotivation

Maslow, whose hierarchy of seven basic needs served as a framework for the development of the Need Theory of Negotiating, is unsparing in his criticism of the present state of moral reasoning. Among the "villains" are:

1. The Freudians, who are "reductionistic about all higher human values. The deepest and most real motivations are seen to be dangerous and nasty, while the highest human values and virtues are

essentially fake, being . . . but camouflaged versions of the deep, dark and dirty."

2. The social scientists, whose doctrine of cultural determinism "not only denies intrinsic higher motivations but comes perilously close . . . to denying 'human nature' itself."

3. The economists, who are essentially materialistic. "[Economics] is generally the skilled, exact technological application of a totally false theory of human needs and values, a theory that recognizes only the existence of lower needs or material needs."

To Maslow's list should be added those who subscribe to the theories of Herbert Spencer, a philosopher who popularized and perverted Charles Darwin's theory of "natural selection" into Social Darwinism and the doctrine of "survival of the fittest." He was a staunch supporter of economic individualism and a foe of social welfare laws, which he felt eliminated the competition that weeds out those unfit for survival. A federal court in 1885 echoed Spencer's moral philosophy while voiding a safety code for New York sweatshops by extolling "the unceasing struggle for success and existence which pervades all societies of men."

These four classes of theorists have several things in common: first and foremost, each espouses highly influential ideas, some of which continue to excite controversy; second, each demands unquestioning obedience from its followers and allows no dissent; third, each class not only accepts, it insists, on a doctrine of limits. Only the favored few are worthy enough to receive the earth's limited resources. Who decides how much each person gets? No one. It is all preordained by moral laws. Even lawyers are not exempt. As one lawyer told the U.S. Supreme Court in 1895: The leaders of the bar are chosen "by a process of natural selection, for merit and fitness, from the whole body of the bar." Anatole France ridiculed these inequities a year earlier: "The law, in its majestic equality, forbids the rich as well as the poor to sleep under bridges, to beg in the streets, and to steal bread."

Today the words may be more guarded but the moral sentiments remain the same: Those individuals (or corporations) who rise only to Kohlberg's stage four are better off since they fit the requirements for modern corporate success. Consider the giant oil company that limits its college and university contributions to the exact sciences because only they can ensure the conservative mindset the company wants in its employees.

We have all seen corporations, such as regulated monopolies, whose policies are dominated by self-imposed limits. They are sober, self-assured and above all stable. A sense of rectitude and order pervades all their decisions. They are models of the static society that the Middle Ages aspired to but never quite achieved. They are a joy to everyone—especially their competitors, deregulations permitting.

Business executives cannot escape from the stress caused by a desire for stability (and limits) on the one hand and the need for growth (and change). It is here that workable ethics can be a soul-saving (and job-saving) benefit. Instead of setting limits ("a few simple rules"), a system of workable ethics is open-ended. Life does not set limits on human potential. Only individuals try to do that. Let's return to Maslow for an example.

Maslow's seven basic needs can be seen as establishing a limit—this far and no further. But once you have satisfied your basic needs, do you stop? Most people do. Maslow offers an alternative:

> By definition, self-actualizing people are gratified in all their basic needs (of belongingness, affection, respect, and self-esteem). This is to say that they have a feeling of belongingness and rootedness, they are satisfied in their love needs, having friends and feeling loved and love-worthy, they have status and place in life and respect from other people, and they have a reasonable feeling of worth and self-respect. If we phrase this negatively, in terms of the frustration of these basic needs and in terms of pathology, then this is to say that self-actualizing people do not (for any length of time) feel anxiety-ridden, insecure, unsafe, do not feel alone, ostracized, rootless, or isolated, do not feel unlovable, rejected or unwanted, do not feel despised and looked down upon, and do not feel deeply unworthy, nor do they have crippling feelings of inferiority or worthlessness.

These people are among those who are securely at stage six of moral reasoning and beyond, and are most likely to be ready to use workable ethics for their own profit and the profit of future generations.

Conclusion

Growth in moral reasoning does not mean rising to a "superior" level. That is merely a prettified version of survival of the fittest. It does mean expanding the scope of your cooperation with others.

It is arguable that the "average" male stops his moral growth at stage four, while the "average" female stops at stage five.

The so-called gender gap can perhaps be closed by all progressing beyond stage six. The self-actualizing level offers views of broader horizons.

VII

Kohlberg's Six Stages of Moral Reasoning

"THE CHILD IS FATHER OF THE Man" wrote Wordsworth, and Kohlberg's six stages illustrate this truth. *The Art of Creative Thinking* gives a detailed analysis of the creative-thinking skills involved in each of the stages of moral reasoning. It also cautions that while a child will progress over a period of time through stage after stage, an adult will simultaneously operate on several levels. Consider that in today's complex business world you may often find yourself operating on different levels (personal, interorganizational, and international) in the course of a single negotiation. In such a situation, it is quite possible that you will understand your operation through all six levels of moral reasoning: You may be aware of yourself functioning on stages three and four of conventional morality, occasionally being forced to operate on stages one and two of pre-conventional morality. However—if you do not want to labor under a severe handicap—you will always reach out to stages five and six of postconventionality and beyond. You should not fault yourself, no matter what level you are presently operating on, but use this insight to understand your potential.

The child, on the other hand, is likely to abandon one stage as he progresses to the next higher one. What rational child, after all, would want to retain the blind fear of stage one when the prospect of maximizing pleasure beckons him on to stage two? Thus the Justice Department report on juvenile delinquency mentioned in chapter 5 does *not* "fly in the face of experience, social science and common sense."

Let's examine the report's findings point by point:

1. While there is some relationship between juvenile delinquency and adult criminality, the relationship is not sufficient to predict adult behavior because juvenile delinquency usually operates on stage two (selfish pleasure) or stage three in the form of loyalty to a gang. Stage three, however, is transitional. In most cases, gang loyalty eventually gives way to larger groups whose approval is sought by the child. He or she remains at stage three but will eventually move on to stage four.

2. Any relationships between juvenile and adult criminality may be explained by the antiquated operation of the criminal justice system (the threat of swift and stern punishment—an appeal to stage-one morality; or a system of justice that can be manipulated—an appeal to stage-two morality).

3. Youths who hold jobs are more likely to get into trouble than those who don't because stage-two gang members with money have more clout than those who are broke.

4. The problem is "how to integrate delinquents into the larger social systems." The report's statistics indicate, however, that this group comprises only 8 percent of adolescents. The other 92 percent have managed to reach stage four "on their own"; so the problem is "why" not "how"?

Why people move from one stage to another may be explained in part by attributing it to "normal" childhood development. This is

fine for the preconventional and conventional stages but what mo-
tivates people to go still further—to postconventional stages five and
six? Real-life examples of the six stages of moral development may
provide some clues.

STAGE ONE: PUNISHMENT/OBEDIENCE ORIENTATION

In 1983, a 12-year-old Tennessee girl was caught up in a legal struggle
pitting the right of an individual to religious freedom against the
right of society to oversee the welfare of minor children. The girl's
father was a pastor of a small church whose members believed that
only God could heal the sick and that medicine should not be used
to treat illness. It was a classic example of the competing moral claims
of Church and State, and the adults on both sides operated on higher
levels of moral reasoning than stage one. The girl, however, did not.
She, following her father's teaching, refused medical treatment for
cancer because it was "against God's will." Doctors predicted that
without treatment she would die, but, for her, fear of God out-
weighed fear of death.

A lengthy court battle ensued, culminating in a higher court or-
dering chemotherapy for the girl. Before an appeals panel could possibly intervene to stop treatment, the child had received her fifth
dose of chemotherapy and had markedly improved.

How did she react to this offense against her stage-one morality?
The nursing supervisor said: "She's not having any of the usual side
effects. . . . She's eating well, and she just seems to be in better
spirits. She's happy. I don't know why."

How quickly an adult forgets the terror of stage-one morality and
the escape from it that rising to stage two affords!

In terms of time-binding, she put the past into its proper perspective, embraced the present, and could look to the future.

STAGE TWO: INSTRUMENTAL-RELATIVIST ORIENTATION

In 1981, a Towson, Maryland, realtor copped a plea, admitting that he had taken $187,723 in federal rent-subsidy money. Under the agreement, he chose what seemed to be a lesser pain—returning all the money and donating 1,000 hours of public service during his first year of probation rather than serving a five-year prison term. While enjoying his freedom, stage-two reevaluation persuaded him that the "real" pain would be paying back all that money—so he didn't—nor did he work all those hours. He put in only 53 hours in time. He went to prison. After a year, prison seemed a poor alternative, not enough of one to make him want to pay back all that money and work all those hours, but definitely a drag. So he applied for parole. He was turned down. His attorney filed an appeal. The parole board said, "Come back next year."

Some might suggest that he change his ways, go to a higher level— say, stage three—and become a "good little boy," but that unfamiliar way did not appeal to him. Thus, many cling to a particular moral level because of fear, especially fear of the unknown.

In time-binding terms, he "forgets" the past, hates the present, and refuses to face reality in the future.

STAGE THREE: INTERPERSONAL CONCORDANCE ORIENTATION

At this level the approval of close associates is the important thing. Unqualified approval is not essential. "With all your faults I love you still" is good enough for someone at the third stage if that's the best he can get. Another characteristic of stage-three morality is a feeling of "them" against "us." "We" are morally superior. That is what sets "us" apart from "them." An episode in the life of the young Teddy Roosevelt illustrates this point.

A Republican state assemblyman of New York at the time, Roosevelt felt compelled one day to address the assembly Democrats: "There is good and bad in each party, but while the bad predominates in yours, it is the good which predominates in ours!" Roosevelt got bad press on this occasion. One reporter wrote: "When Mr. Roosevelt had finished his affecting oration, the House was in tears—of uncontrollable laughter."

A hundred years later (March 1, 1982), the *New York Times* reported an alternative to this "good guys versus bad guys" vision of life. It might be termed the "if they don't say it's good, it isn't necessarily bad" ethical principle. The story had to do with Securities and Exchange commissioners who overruled an S.E.C.'s enforcement staff recommendation. The staff wanted the commission to bring an action against Citicorp for inadequate disclosure of its foreign currency trading practices. One of the arguments advanced by the commissioners: corporations have minimal obligation to disclose illegal conduct, especially where management has never represented that it has "honesty and integrity." The *Times* did not mention whether anyone laughed or even smiled at this ethical milestone.

Considered in time-binding terms, when a person is at stage three, the present is all that matters.

STAGE FOUR: LAW AND ORDER ORIENTATION

An editorial in the *New York Post* (August 29, 1983) took an uncompromising law-and-order stance:

> New York City isn't the only city fighting crime and hooliganism, but how differently do the Chinese Communists make the punishment fit the crime.
> Buses and trucks brought 100,000 people to the Peking Workers' Stadium on Tuesday to hear Mayor Chen Xitong proclaim the need to preserve public order. They then cheered in unison as 29 men and a woman—convicted of murders, rape, arson and theft—were hauled

off to be executed by a single pistol shot, Chinese style, in the back of the head.

No plea bargaining! No lawyers!

In time-binding terms, you destroy the evil past in a vain hope that that will make for a better present—but the future will be uncertain.

In moral education, as in other areas of human development, some people reach a certain stage or level and remain there for the rest of their lives. Some are content with the plateau they have reached and see no point in changing. Others are dissatisfied but feel that they lack the skills that are needed to reach a more mature stage of development and involve a larger number of people. It is the intention of this book to add to their skills.

The first group—the contented or complacent—are moral-education dropouts and deserve only a passing glance. An example: A senior partner of John Muir & Company, a brokerage firm that collapsed some years ago creating heavy losses for its investors, boasted: "If I don't work another day in my life, I figure I have made a major contribution to the capitalist system."

An example of those who are dissatisfied and unfulfilled is U.S. President Grover Cleveland. In the 19th century, no deathbed scene was complete without a scribe recording the "famous last words" of notable men (and, occasionally, women). Cleveland's were: "I have tried so hard to do right."

Whether or not Cleveland actually said that, it neatly sums up the driving force of his life. The hidden meaning of the words would seem to be that no matter how faithfully he followed his own rigid sense of right and wrong, he got little peace from it. Neither, for that matter, did members of political factions and other special interest groups that encountered him. As governor of New York and later during his two nonconsecutive terms as U.S. president, he managed to alienate virtually every group that offended his stage-four standards. Society's need for law and order determined the course of all his public actions.

In the book *The Rise of Theodore Roosevelt* (New York: Coward, McCann & Geoghegan, Inc., 1979), Edmund Morris gives a vivid description of Cleveland's style:

So potent was his [Cleveland's] image as a man of brutal honesty and toughness that even Roosevelt's own staunchly Republican district had voted for him. . . . The Governor was invariably patient and courteous; his first official announcement had been that his door was open to all comers. Yet the slightest appeal to favor, as opposed to justice, would cause the dark eyes to narrow, and evoke a menacing rumble from somewhere behind the walrus mustache: "I don't know that I understand you." Should a foolhardy petitioner blunder on, the sack of cement [Cleveland] would suddenly heave and sway, and a ponderous fist crash down on the nearest surface, signifying that the interview was over.

Since the "nearest surface" was often Cleveland's arthritic knee, the result could be spectacular.

Cleveland's political life is a pristine example of stage-four morality. As governor and later as president he seemed to believe that he— and possibly only he—could act as the stern and righteous judge of what was "right" or "wrong." In contrast to that of many politicians of his day, his incorruptible stand on law and order won him a wide following. (He got a majority of the popular vote in three presidential elections but lost the 1888 election in the Electoral College.) Why, then, did he finally seem doubtful about whether or not he had "done right"?

One reason surely is that he used his ethical principles as a club rather than a tool for relating to others. During his eight years as president, his accomplishments were relatively few, and many of his actions alienated his natural supporters. At no time did he seem to consider the needs of people, only his strict, unchanging sense of right and wrong.

A final example of Cleveland's staunch support of stage-four morality involved the young Teddy Roosevelt, who was to follow in Cleveland's footsteps, becoming governor of New York and ultimately president of the United States. While still in the New York Assembly, Roosevelt labored mightily to get a series of reform bills through the legislature, only to learn that Cleveland planned to veto them unless all the i's were dotted and the t's crossed. Roosevelt argued passionately that details were unimportant, only the "principle" mattered. "You must not veto those bills," Roosevelt cried. "You cannot. You shall not. . . . I won't have it."

Cleveland's fist crashed down. "Mr. Roosevelt, I'm going to veto those bills!"

In time-binding terms, Cleveland sought to make the present so perfect there would be no need to change in the future. His actions reveal how stage-four moral principles fall short when viewed in relation to time-binding.

STAGE FIVE: SOCIAL CONTRACT/RATIONAL ORIENTATION

Roosevelt's unfortunate run-in with Cleveland indicates that the younger politician was in transition and attempting to operate on the stage-five level. On this level, the goal is a consensus reached by rival groups in a pluralistic society. The rigidly held principles of stage four are abandoned. Instead of ironclad rules, the stage-five moralist believes that laws can reach a consensus, not so much for the "safety of the people" but for the "good" of everyone. What the laws are is less important than what they do or do not accomplish.

A celebrated stage-five moralist was Henry Clay, that 19th-century prototype of Harold Stassen—the perennial candidate for U.S. president. Clay is chiefly remembered for two things: his nickname and a quotation. In 1850, after his last unsuccessful try for the presidency, he uttered a bit of sour-grapes meta-talk: "I'd rather be right than be President." What he felt he was "right" about was the Compromise of 1850, one of his many attempts to avert war between the North and South over the issue of slavery. This and earlier attempts won him the nickname, "The Great Compromiser."

For many voters at that time, this was high praise indeed. He was also admired for his philosophy of government. In brief: "All society is founded upon the principle of mutual concession, politeness, comity, courtesy. . . ."

Clay applied his philosophy to negotiate what was then regarded as his greatest achievement, the Missouri Compromise of 1820. This act helped postpone the Civil War by admitting Maine to the Union as a free state and Missouri as a slave state. Clay examined his creation from his stage-five height and saw that it was good. However, Thomas Jefferson, on the sixth level, disagreed:

> This momentous question, like a fire bell in the night, awakened and filled me with terror. I considered it at once as the knell of the Union. It is hushed, indeed, for the moment. But this is a reprieve only, not a final sentence. A geographical line, coinciding with a marked principle, moral and political, once conceived and held up to the angry passions of men, will never be obliterated; and every new irritation will mark it deeper and deeper.

Which one was "right"? Both of them. Each accomplished what he could by operating on the highest level he was capable of. Clay's efforts postponed the Civil War for about 40 years. Jefferson's prophecy was fulfilled and the divisions he warned of are still felt today. However, Jefferson was then an elder statesman, long since gone from the White House. The Sage of Monticello could not lead the nation, and Clay and other leaders did not have the vision to lead the nation to a settlement beneficial to all. A stage-five compromise could conceal but not "bind up the nation's wounds." That task was left for a later, stage-six moral leader.

In time-binding terms, Clay, living in the past, could see no further than the present. The future was vague and menacing, populated with the ghosts of postponed problems, as Jefferson rightly recognized.

STAGE SIX: UNIVERSAL ETHICAL PRINCIPLE ORIENTATION—A PROTOTYPE OF WORKABLE ETHICS

With the wry wit he was famous for, President John F. Kennedy once told a gathering of American Nobel Prize winners that more talent and genius was present at the White House that evening than had ever been since Thomas Jefferson last dined there alone. None of the Nobel Prize laureates seem to have disagreed with this assessment of their considerable, but circumscribed, achievements. Indeed, it would be difficult to find Jefferson's match in any age. Scientist, philosopher, educator, pioneer in scientific farming, architect, musician, writer, inventor—these were some of his talents. His list of achievements is even longer. Indeed, he makes Maslow's self-actualizing people seem like underachievers.

But, business executives whose "corporate brains are getting warning flashes from their noncorporate brains" might ask, "Did Jefferson find the time to be a moralist too?" Indeed he did—and most notably in great matters of state. (Possible moral lapses in his private life we leave to revisionist historians and muckrakers.) His achievements require detailed analysis.

An instructive example is the Louisiana Purchase, his chief accomplishment as president. Even before his inauguration in 1801, rumors had spread that Spain was about to cede Louisiana back to France. In spite of his long-standing admiration of France, Jefferson said there was "on the globe one single spot, the possessor of which is our natural and habitual enemy. It is New Orleans through which the produce of three-eighths of our territory must pass to market. . . ."

The next year (1802) the cession of Louisiana to France was confirmed and Jefferson immediately initiated negotiations with France for the purchase of New Orleans. Napoleon in a counteroffer said he was willing to sell the entire territory. Jefferson was all for the purchase, but as a strict constructionist (and operating at stage four), he questioned whether the Constitution permitted it. He would have preferred an amendment to the Constitution to make the transaction clearly legal, but there seemed to be a strong possibility that Napoleon might try to back out of the deal. So, going up to stage six, Jefferson settled for Senate ratification of the treaty.

A footnote to the above: Jefferson at first did not mind that Spain held New Orleans. It was too weak to resist U.S. pressure. A strong France under Napoleon was a different story. Once a deal with France had been negotiated, however, Spain considered holding it up by refusing to retrocede the territory. Acting again at stage four, Jefferson sent troops to the border. This show of force persuaded Spain to respect international "law and order" and Louisiana became U.S. territory.

The above account is necessarily limited to a brief summary of an enormously complex international situation, but it affords several examples of Jefferson's creative use of morality:

Was the purchase moral? Some American historians would say no: "Seemingly Jefferson's conscience was not in the least troubled by what Napoleon Bonaparte had done. That unscrupulous ruler had sold Louisiana to the United States in direct contravention of a provision in the French constitution, and he had also violated his pledge to Spain never to sell Louisiana to a third power. . . . In a sense the United States had acted as the receiver of stolen goods. Bonaparte required the cession of Louisiana from Spain because Spain could not stand up to him, and he sold Louisiana to the United States in order to get money for his impending war against Great Britain. Viewed from any angle it was a disreputable proceeding, *but it proved to be of vast importance to the United States, whose territory was expanded by the purchase not less than 140 percent."* (Italics ours.) (John D. Hicks, George E. Mowry, Robert E. Burke, *The Federal Union*, Boston: Houghton Mifflin Company, 1970).

Korzybski would emphatically disagree with those American historians' static moral judgment. A relevant passage has already been quoted: "In recent civilization, ethics, because controlled by theology and law, which are static, could not duly influence the dynamic, revolutionary progress of technique. . . . Medieval legalism and medieval morals . . . being by their nature . . . opposed to change [are] becoming more and more unable to support the mighty social burden of the modern world."

In any event, history, if not some historians, is likely to forgive Jefferson's lack of "moral" qualms.

Did Jefferson think his action was morally right? Absolutely. Indeed it seems ironic that he should be accused of being an accomplice in violating the French constitution and in ignoring France's "sacred" promises. While minister to France, Jefferson had been intimately involved in the French revolutionary movement. He witnessed and cheered the fall of the Bastille, helped Lafayette draft his Declaration of the Rights of Man, and felt the mob execution of Bastille officers had had a therapeutic effect on the king, who "went to bed fearfully impressed." With incurable optimism he expected a peaceful evolution into a constitutional monarchy. Instead, he had to deal with the dictator Napoleon, who not only had violated promises to Spain but also to the French people, promises that Jefferson remembered quite well. The moral principle that Jefferson adhered to was quite clear:

> The earth belongs always to the living generation. They may manage it then, and what proceeds from it as they please, during their usufruct. They are masters too of their own persons, and consequently may govern them as they please.

As president, Jefferson felt his moral obligation was to present and future American generations, not to the European past. A central concern of his was that if New Orleans fell into hostile hands, the settlers in the territory west of the 13 original colonies might secede from the Union and would almost certainly attempt to seize New Orleans. Therefore, Jefferson chose to lead, rather than let events lead him. Even traditional moralists approved of that much of the bargain.

A final comment on Jefferson's use of time-binding: According to the record, Jefferson had bought a pig in a poke, for he had purchased an undefined territory, whose vague boundaries were to be the same "that it now has in the hands of Spain and that it had when France possessed it." Since vast portions of the territory were unknown to most U.S. citizens, Jefferson felt free to claim all territory not settled by European settlers.

Then, as now, the inclination of traditional moralists was to postpone the consideration of a problem until a resolution of it was absolutely necessary. Then each side, rising to stage five, would advance its own version of what was "morally right." This would be followed by a compromise satisfying no one but putting off a "final" solution in which each side would give up at least something.

Jefferson's mind did not work that way. Long before he became president he had had an avid desire to know more about the geography, and the flora and fauna of the regions outside the boundaries of the United States. As president, he began planning an expedition, the goals of which were to discover a water route across the continent, establish a U.S. claim to the Oregon Territory, and secure friendly relations with the Indians of the Northwest, which would be indispensable in the development of trade. After a year of preparation, the Lewis and Clark expedition was launched; it arrived in St. Louis in time to receive the formal transfer of the upper Louisiana Territory to the United States.

These interrelated examples of Jefferson's mind at work help to illuminate the difference between the traditional moralist, depending on metaphysical rules, and the creative moralist, relying on the scientific method. The former would possibly condemn Jefferson's acts and attribute their success to accident or fool's luck. The latter might very well see them as the products of an unfettered, creative mind. Jefferson is certainly a prototype of the use of workable ethics. Korzybski, in defining human engineering, could have had him in mind: The "science and art of so directing human energies and capacities as to make them contribute most effectively to the advancement of human welfare." In his finest moments Jefferson acted on Kohlberg's sixth stage of moral reasoning, was a persuasive example of Maslow's self-actualizing human being, and proceeded according to Korzybski's concept of human engineering. His workable ethics produced enduring benefits to mankind that are felt to this day.

A further examination of his reaction to Henry Clay's Compromise of 1820 may help to clarify the difference between traditional and creative morality. Jefferson believed the compromise was an abomination. "A geographical line" (the so-called Mason-Dixon line) would serve to divide the country, even though traditional moralists saw it as the nation's salvation. Jefferson had a more than casual interest in the matter. The compromise extended the Mason-Dixon line, which had been the boundary between Pennsylvania, a free state, and Maryland, a slave state, westward, thus dividing the Louisiana Territory into slave and free land. Jefferson was sure this political and moral boundary could not endure and it didn't.

Thomas Roderick Drew, a Southern professor of metaphysics, offered this defense of slavery in 1832: "It is the order of nature and of God that the being of superior facilities and knowledge, and therefore of superior power, should control and dispose of those who are inferior. It is as much the order of nature that men should enslave each other as that other animals should prey upon each other." Thus Drew perniciously applies, as Herbert Spencer would, the theory of "survival of the fittest" to society.

Did Jefferson, as a creative moralist, have a "better" solution? Unquestionably he did. In 1784, he was the author of an ordinance providing for the Northwest Territory (comprising Ohio, Illinois, Indiana, Michigan and Wisconsin) to enter the Union as free territory. It eventually was adopted with modifications in 1787. Years later those five states played a crucial role in preserving the Union during the Civil War.

It should be noted that Jefferson opposed slavery on moral grounds. His impassioned attack on the "peculiar institution," which he included in his draft of the Declaration of Independence, was deleted by more "practical" politicians, but his opposition continued throughout his life. Some historians claim that Jefferson's ban on slavery in the Northwest Territory was "merely" to attract New England settlers to the territory. Otherwise, their opposition to slavery would prevent their coming. Even if this were the only reason, it is powerful proof of workable ethics at work. To adopt a worthy cause that produces lasting benefits for all mankind should be the aim of all.

CONCLUSION

Moral development often occurs by a natural progression: Each step upward, until stage four is reached, is easier to make—but only at the cost of conformity to society's demands.

Being good is not as good as being good for something.

Compromises seldom produce satisfactory, enduring agreements. Some compromises are reached by making mutual concessions. Others result in the compromising and yielding of moral principles.

Reaching and going beyond stage six, moralists should not regard individuals as animals and/or gods, but as members of a time-binding class, aware of their debt to the past and conscious of their obligation to the future.

CHAPTER
VIII

A Look Backwards—Thinking the Unthinkable

> Soviet-American relations have reached one of the lowest points in a generation as the two nations trade recriminations over the Middle East, Central America, Afghanistan and missile deployments in Europe, according to many Government and academic specialists.
>
> The specialists regard the three years since the Soviet intervention in Afghanistan in December 1979 as a time of protracted tension, sharp and acrimonious charges, diplomatic stalemate and mutual suspicion. Soviet visitors as well as American officials speak warily of the prospects for "doing business" with the other side.
>
> —HEDRICK SMITH, *New York Times*, May 24, 1983

THE PROTAGONISTS MAY CHANGE and the "holy" causes may vary, but throughout the ages people have sometimes been confronted with the need to "do business" with others whom they fear, hate or regard as morally repugnant. Short of war or stalemate, there seems to be no viable alternative. Can there be a way that is not immoral and/or self-defeating?

The Games that Harvard Plays

First, let's examine the state of the art of "doing business" as practiced by a very influential group of American business executives today.

In *Life and Death on the Corporate Battlefield* (New York: Simon and Schuster, 1982), Paul Solman and Thomas Friedman take a close look at the Harvard Graduate School of Business Administration:

> In the M.B.A. program, students learn not only lessons of logic, analysis, and procedure, but also how to develop a killer instinct. Self-interest dominates the classwork, which features competitive games. . . . [One] second-year M.B.A. elective [is] called Competitive Decision Making, in which the class plays thirty competitive games in the course of the term. One-third of each student's grade is based on how well he or she fares in the competition. Competitive game playing—and winning—is a very serious business here.

The course is based on John von Neumann's Game Theory. A game consists of a set of rules governing a competitive situation in which individuals or groups employ strategies designed to maximize their own winnings. It is assumed that every player is out to "win" and that arbitrarily chosen numbers can indicate the costs and payoffs of any given strategy. (See Appendix A for a detailed analysis.)

A close look at the Harvard Business School, where the rules are what the professors say they are, provides a context for understanding the introductory quotation about Soviet-American relations. Stage-two morality, whether on the interpersonal, interorganizational or international level, offers too little space for mature human relationships to thrive and develop. "We" are inside the circle of wagons. "They" are on the outside ready to attack. And attack they will. There is something about the moral philosophy of maximizing pleasure and minimizing pain that prompts even your most civilized adversary to try to maximize *your* pain and minimize *your* pleasure.

The noted anthropologist and social biologist Ashley Montagu provides a splendid example of what can happen when a stage-two moralist collides with the "real" world. In a letter to the *New York Times*, dated May 31, 1983, he said:

> Dr. Robert Ackerman's criticism of your endorsement of the bill pending before the New York State Legislature which would allow the nurse-practioner to handle "simple medical problems" is ill-founded.
>
> Dr. Ackerman says, "There is no such entity as 'simple medical problems' that do not require examination by a thoroughly trained

physician." The fact is that many, perhaps most, problems that come to medical attention are quite simple, easily diagnosed and effectively treatable by any appropriately trained individual.

One of the most serious defects in medical training is the built-in tendency to perceive the patient as presenting a condition that requires, as Dr. Ackerman so engagingly puts it, "the profound depths of medical knowledge." The truth is that most conditions with which the physician is confronted require no knowledge that is beyond the grasp of any intelligent human. Hence, as an old medical school teacher, I very much hope that the bill will receive speedy passage.

With a final pat of his shovel, Dr. Montagu adds:

> Finally, may I congratulate you on the illustration accompanying Dr. Ackerman's letter, showing the correct form of the medical caduceus, the staff with *one* snake, rather than the two so frequently and erroneously displayed by those in any way connected with medicine. That is the emblem of Hermes or Mercury, god of commerce, invention, cunning and theft, who also served as herald for the other gods, patron of travelers and rogues and conductor of the dead to Hades.

I'm Just a Prisoner (There Is a Way Out)

Even a novice would probably recognize the Game Theory matrix described in the Appendix as a variation on the Prisoner's Dilemma, a paradox discovered about 1950 by Merril M. Flood and Melvin Dresher. For the business school instructor the "logical" (but losing) move would be for the players each to chose A2 and B2 and lose $2. The "winning" game would net $10 for one player and a loss of $5 for the other. All of this, of course, takes place within the narrow confines of stage-two morality. Is it possible to go beyond that to later stages of moral development and still "win"?

Douglas R. Hofstadter in "Metamagical Themas" (*Scientific American*, July 1983, pp. 16–26) believes it *is* possible. In a variation of the game, two dealers agree to exchange commodities by one leaving a bag at a designated place in the woods while the other dealer leaves his bag at another designated place. They then pick up their new bags and see what they have got. Has the other cooperated (left a full bag) or defected (left an empty bag)? Hofstadter comments:

> Clearly there is a something for each of you to fear, namely that the other will leave an empty bag. Obviously if you both leave full bags, you both will be satisfied, but equally obviously it is even more satisfying to get something for nothing. You are therefore tempted to leave an empty bag. In fact, you can even reason it through with seeming rigor this way. "If the dealer brings a full bag, I'll be better off having left an empty bag, because I'll have got all I wanted and given away nothing. If the dealer brings an empty bag, I'll be better off having left an empty bag because I'll not have been cheated. . . ." The dealer thinks analogous thoughts and comes to the parallel conclusion. . . . And so both of you, with your impeccable (or seemingly impeccable) logic, leave empty bags and go away empty-handed. How sad, because if you both had just cooperated, you could each have gained something you wanted to have.

This last sentence rather wistfully implies what is morally "wrong" with Prisoner's Dilemma games as they are played and interpreted at Harvard. They are firmly rooted in preconventional morality—particularly at stage two. "How sad" signals a desire to shift from the egocentric moral child to stages three and four, which focus outward to the needs and expectations of society. Clearly society benefits when instead of the winner taking all, or each gaining nothing, both have gained something they wanted.

At first glance, Korzybski's concept of humanity as the time-binding class of life seems totally unrelated to competitive game playing at the Harvard Graduate School of Business Administration. There is a relationship, but it is necessary to remember two hoary concepts that are still firmly entrenched in many areas of modern business life. The first is the medieval belief that mankind is part animal (the space-binding class according to Korzybski) and part supernatural—something that can be known only through a priori reasoning. The other outmoded concept is the familiar "survival of the fittest" doctrine. Together they produce the amoral philosophy, "Play to win and be sure there's a loser."

Much of Hofstadter's article is based on *The Evolution of Cooperation*

(New York: Basic Books, 1984) by Robert Axelrod, a professor of political science at the University of Michigan and a research scientist at the Institute for Public Policy Studies, Ann Arbor. Axelrod was earlier joined by William D. Hamilton, an evolutionary biologist, in working out and publishing a series of revolutionary findings that stand conventional evolutionary theory on its head and clear the way for the use of creative morality as envisioned by Korzybski.

Axelrod and Hamilton's first major article on this work was the prize-winning "The Evolution of Cooperation" (*Science*, March 27, 1981, Vol. 212, No. 4489, pp. 1390–1396). It began:

> The theory of evolution is based on the struggle for life and the survival of the fittest. Yet cooperation is common between members of the same species and even between members of different species. Before about 1960, accounts of the evolutionary process largely dismissed cooperative phenomena as not requiring special attention. This position followed from a misreading of theory that assigned most adaptation to selection at the level of populations or whole species. As a result of such misreading, cooperation was always considered adaptive. Recent reviews of the evolutionary process, however, have shown no sound basis for a pervasive group benefit view of selection; at the level of a species or a population, the process of selection is weak. *The original individualistic emphasis of Darwin's theory is more valid* [italics added].

Not only does the article demolish a cherished tenet of the typical Harvard M.B.A.—"Nature, red in tooth and claw"—it uses the very same techniques the instructors have used to teach the concept. In both, the Prisoner's Dilemma plays a central part in determinations of "winners." Both agree that "while an individual can benefit by mutual cooperation, each one can do even better by exploiting the cooperative efforts of others." Hence the cutthroat game at Harvard where there may occasionally be a winner and loser but, more often than not, two losers. Axelrod and Hamilton present a matrix of the Prisoner's Dilemma game that is somewhat more sophisticated than the one presented earlier. (See Appendix B.)

In conclusion, Axelrod states:

> *With two individuals destined never to meet again* [italics added], the only strategy that can be called a solution to the game is to defect always. . . .

Apart from being the solution in game theory, defection is also the solution in biological evolution. It is the outcome of inevitable evolutionary trends through mutation and natural selection: If the payoffs are in terms of fitness, and the interactions between pairs of individuals are random and not repeated, then any population with a mixture of heritable strategies evolves to a state where all individuals are defectors. Moreover, no single differing mutant strategy can do better than others when the population is using this strategy. In these respects the strategy of defection is stable.

At Harvard, and in Axelrod and Hamilton's article, two games are played: (1) in one, the players meet only once, and (2) in the other, the players meet a specified number of times. In either of these cases the strategy of defection is "best" because a population of individuals cannot be invaded by a rare mutant adopting a different strategy. This, incidentally, is one reason why stage-four morality has such a powerful hold on a majority of the population. It provides an impregnable defense against all invaders. As a side effect, it is evolutionarily stable. Change is neither desired nor achieved.

But what if the game model were based on the more realistic assumption that the number of interactions were not fixed and that the same individuals would meet again and again? Then it would be a whole new "game." Then the unthinkable is not only possible but probable. Both individuals *can* win. Advanced stages of morality *can* be put to practical and constructive use. The time-binding ability of mankind *can* be effectively harnessed.

Free at Last

Many of the benefits sought by living things are disproportionally available to cooperating groups. While there are considerable differences in what is meant by the terms "benefits" and "sought," this statement, insofar as it is true, lays down a fundamental basis for all social life (Axelrod and Hamilton).

To stage-four moralists seeking limited cooperation, this credo probably smacks of heresy. It certainly goes against past traditional wisdom and common sense, not to mention competitive game-playing assumptions. Furthermore, the authors are not content to stop there. They assert that an organism does not even need a brain to play the same games as they do at Harvard. They offer these points:

1. Bacteria are highly responsive to certain aspects of their environment (e.g., chemicals).

2. They probably can respond differentially to the actions of other organisms near them.

3. These responses can be inherited.

4. A bacterium can have an affect on other nearby organisms just as they can have an affect on it.

Not having a brain, however, has its drawbacks. Bacteria cannot "remember" or "interpret" complex past sequences of changes or, as Korzybski would say, they are space-binding, not time-binding. That quality is found much further up the evolutionary ladder, but each rung up permits richer, more creative game-playing behavior. On the human level, these improvements are possible:

1. Experience and the memory of it permits a continuing evaluation of interactions in a process world.

2. This allows more accurate judgments of whether or not the same individual will be encountered again.

3. It discriminates among the individuals encountered, allowing a rational (and moral) choice of conduct. In terms of the Prisoner's Dilemma game, it enables you to decide how to behave—cooperate or defect—based on the same Game Theory data as others use but viewed from a different stage of moral development. Thus, no one "gets socked." Everybody wins.

With the insights provided by Axelrod and Hamilton, is it possible to evolve a strategy that will yield a payoff for both sides? Remembering that there is "no assumption of commensurability of payoffs between the two sides," but that the payoffs satisfy the conditions set forth in the Prisoner's Dilemma, the authors believe that the evolution is not only possible but desirable. They pose three questions to test the viability of various strategies:

1. *Robustness*. What type of strategy can thrive in a variegated environment composed of others using a wide variety of more or less sophisticated strategies?

2. *Stability*. Under what conditions can such a strategy, once fully established, resist invasion by mutant strategies?

3. *Initial viability*. Even if a strategy is robust and stable, how can it ever get a foothold in an environment which is predominantly noncooperative?

To see what single strategy can thrive in a variegated environment, Axelrod conducted a computer tournament for the Prisoner's Dilemma. Unlike Harvard Business School, Axelrod's tournament did not place a high evaluation on one organism "beating" another or even how many "victories" one had. The true test of the efficacy of a particular strategy was the *total point count* tallied up on a series of encounters with other organisms over an extended period of time. A careful reading of Axelrod's *The Evolution of Cooperation* is recommended, but the program that won was the shortest of all programs submitted: TIT FOR TAT submitted by Anatol Rapaport, the mathematician and general semanticist. Its very simple tactic is: Cooperate on the first move, thereafter do whatever the other player did on the previous move. That is all there is to it. Or is it?

CONCLUSION

Grantland Rice penned the famous couplet "When the One Great Scorer comes to write against your name, He marks not that you won or lost, but how you played the game." It was published in

Alumnus Football. Could it be that Harvard gentlemen who play football rank higher on the ethics scoreboard than those seeking M.B.A.'s?

The use of mankind's time-binding capacity permits self-actualizing people to capitalize on the wisdom of the past and present to build a better future.

A strategy that is robust, stable and initially viable can produce cooperation that is beneficial to all. How? By harnessing the time-binding capacity to produce a morally good and beneficial conclusion.

Time-binding is ideally suited for dealing with the process world. It provides continuity, yet promotes change as a desirable moral goal.

CHAPTER
IX

Tests for Power, Morality and Time-Binding

IN HIS OLD AGE, John Adams wrote to his friend Thomas Jefferson: "Power always thinks it has a great soul and vast views beyond the comprehension of the weak; and that it is doing God's service when it is violating all His laws."

Adams and Jefferson, both consummate politicians, had learned from bitter experience that a moral consensus in the political arena is often achieved at the expense of political *and* religious freedom. For example, those who perform abortions and those who bomb abortion clinics both can find political and religious leaders who support the morality of their actions. At the same time, Congressman Barney Frank could (and did) describe the Reagan administration's concern for American children as beginning with conception and ending with birth.

Suffer, Little Children

To be fair, Frank's statement is not quite true. Of course, the Physician Task Force on Hunger in America found in February, 1985, that more than 20 million Americans went hungry at least two days a month due to cuts in federal food programs and that children were found to be suffering from diseases caused by severe protein and calorie deprivation—diseases not seen in the United States in many years. The administration, however, did display great concern that infants might be allowed to die of a "treatable" birth defect.

In April, 1985, Margaret M. Heckler, the secretary of health and human services, released regulations covering cases in which infants with severe or multiple handicaps may be allowed to die through denial of medical care. Only three cases were permitted:

1.   An infant is chronically and irreversibly comatose.

2.   Treatment would merely prolong an inevitable death. (Whatever that may mean. Most people would concede that death is *always* inevitable.)

3.   Treatment is so extreme and so likely to be futile that it becomes inhumane to administer it.

Heckler claimed that the rule "reflects the need to establish a careful balance between the need to establish effective protection of the rights of disabled infants and the need to avoid unreasonable governmental intrusion into the practice of medicine and parental responsibilities."

This last statement is so cynical that one would have to go back to Jonathan Swift's pamphlet *A Modest Proposal* (1729) to find its equal. In it, Swift suggested a way to end famine in Ireland: the children of the poor should be sold as food, for the tables of the rich. The only "parental responsibility" proposed by Heckler would be for them to pay the medical bills without complaint (and certainly without government "handouts" since Medicaid funds had been cut).

What would be their "reward"? Columnist Dorothy Gilliam, who often writes about the problems of blacks and women, wrote a column about a woman on welfare who had such difficulty feeding her four children that she often went without food herself. Some of the responses Gilliam received from readers indicated, she said, that Americans in the mid-1980's had "lost not only compassion, but even tolerance for the poor." Examples:

> "What do you black niggers expect, welfare from cradle to grave?"
> "White Americans are fed up with the inferior black."
> "Why don't [you blacks] with ample income start a program to educate these 'poor blacks' to not having so many illegitimate children? . . . Stop writing about the poor blacks and get out and do something to help them into a mood to correct their status."
> "There is an old saying that you can take a pig out of the mud, dress him up, give him a bath, and spray him with perfume. But once he is let out, he will go right back to his old familiar surroundings, wallowing in the mud. The same can be said for the kind of people you and your left-wingers continue to support."

The High Cost of Defending the Innocent

In contrast, U.S. Attorney General Edwin Meese III and his defense lawyers set an example for "welfare cheats." Instead of feeding at the public trough for a lifetime, they dipped but once and presumably would be satisfied. On April 15, 1985, the lawyers submitted a detailed listing of fees and expenses for defending Meese on each of 12 issues charging violations of the Ethics in Government Act. An independent counsel had found no basis for bringing charges against Meese, who gained Senate confirmation as attorney general and the right to be reimbursed by the taxpayers for legal expenses.

Appropriately, American taxpayers learned on April 15 the price they were expected to pay for the vindication of a high public servant. Total fee, $720,924, broken down as follows:

> An allegation that Meese had failed to disclose a $15,000 loan to his wife from one of his aides
>
> $155,858.75

An allegation that the sale of Meese's California home was connected with a federal job given to the man who arranged the loan
(legal fees)   127,213.75
(expenses)   9,005.36

An allegation that loans to Meese were arranged by a man who was later appointed to the U.S. Postal Board of Governors
(legal fees)   101,397.50
(expenses)   6,799.20

An allegation that Meese received preferential treatment when he was promoted in the U.S. Army Reserve
(legal fees)   95,537.50
(expenses)   5,707.20

An allegation that Meese improperly received a $10,000 check from the Presidential Transition Trust
(legal fees)   66,385.00
(expenses)   6,009.80

An allegation that he had received cuff links worth more than $140 from a foreign government
(legal fees)   6,070.00
(expenses)   369.84

There is a sequel to this story: Happily for Meese, but no consolation to the taxpayer, he reported that he had not required the services of his expensive law firms during 10 of the 11 investigations conducted *before* an independent counsel was appointed. He would have been personally responsible for any such legal fees. However, on the eleventh investigation, into allegations that he and his wife had engaged in insider trading (which preceded the special investigator's probe by "a matter of days"), one of the two law firms that defended him later—at taxpayers' expense—said it was a freebie for Meese. Who says lawyers don't have hearts?

The World According to Gardner

Unfortunately, those handicapped children "saved" by Heckler and a "compassionate" government, did not fare well. Two days after

Meese's bills came in and Heckler issued her rules, Senator Lowell P. Weicker, Jr., revealed a vision of the future for handicapped children conjured up by Eileen Marie Gardner, a special assistant for educational philosophy and practice to Education Secretary William J. Bennett. Gardner, in what might loosely be termed a seminal policy paper written for the Heritage Foundation, set forth a "philosophy" that Weicker found to be the "most incredible thing I've ever read. . . . I've never seen such a callousness as long as I have been here in Washington." The Senator may have been more sensitive than most because his son was born with Down's syndrome.

Among the bad seeds scattered by Gardner were these:

"The handicapped constituency displays a strange lack of concern for the effects of their regulations upon the welfare of the general population.

"Although the handicapped constituency has experienced some curtailment of its increasingly unreasonable demands, overall it seems to be experiencing a great deal of success attaining its ends.

"The success of the handicapped constituency at the federal level was impressive. It had money, 'deep conviction' and little opposition. It seemed to occupy the high moral ground which few could bring themselves to oppose.

"The proper role of the federal government in education is no role. It was never intended that the federal government become involved in this domain. Education is not mentioned in the U. S. Constitution.

"There is no justice in the universe. As unfair as it may seem, a person's external circumstances do fit his level of inner spiritual development. The purpose (and the challenge) of life is for a person to take what he has and to use it for spiritual growth. Those of the handicapped constituency who seek to have others bear their burdens and eliminate their challenges are seeking to avoid the central issues of their lives.

"The order in the universe is composed of different degrees of development. There is a higher (more advanced) development and a lower (less advanced). . . . Man cannot, then, within one short life span and from without, raise the lower to meet the higher. Because performance depends on evolution, the only way the performance of the lower can be made equal to that of the higher is artificially to constrain and pervert the performance of the higher. . . . This artificial constrainment is exactly what has happened over the past two decades."

In defending Gardner from Weicker's attack, Bennett had the chutzpah to say the senator had indulged in "character assassination" and charged that he was ridiculing Gardner's "religious" beliefs. One is reminded of that 1920's classic *Gentlemen Prefer Blondes*, in which the heroine's girlfriend says, "Lady, you could no more ruin this girl's reputation than you could sink the Jewish fleet." Committing political hara-kiri is not "character assassination."

Although social Darwinism and other forms of human sacrifice have occasionally been linked to religious beliefs—the quaint customs of the Aztecs come to mind—few would argue that they stem from God's laws. Bennett, after sleeping on the matter, came to the same conclusion. The day after Gardner's testimony, Bennett accepted her resignation with unconcealed relief.

What, if anything, is immoral about Gardner's philosophical stance? "Bleeding hearts" would find it a real tearjerker. Stage-one moralists would regard it as the voice of authority. Stage-two moralists would agree with her—so long as they were not included. Stage-three moralists would join one of the two packs. Stage-four types would, if they thought about it, face a dilemma. The dirty little secret of the whole situation was that the Reagan administration wanted to abolish the Education Department but Congress didn't. Bennett and other appointees were hired to denounce the whole idea of a Department of Education. Law and order anyone? (After all, the department had been established by law.)

Stage-five moralists would (and did) scurry around trying to "save" the Education Department while lobotomizing it. The money in its budget was just too good for politicians to pass up.

Stage-six moralists might take note of a *Washington Post* editorial suggesting that Gardner's post, created just for her, was "the kind of pretentious boon-doggling that serious intellectuals correctly deride. . . . Abolishing it deserves at least as much consideration as, say, another cut in the school lunch money."

Self-actualizing people might want to take a look at future generations, handicapped or not: After all, they are going to be saddled with the obscene national debt now being piled up. They will need all the help they can get, even enough education so they can afford to pay taxes.

Here again we can see the inadequacy of Kohlberg's six stages of moral reasoning. They indicate how we may be good and perhaps even better. But they do not tell us how to be good for something. Korzybski, on the other hand, provides us with a method of evaluation called time-binding, which links past, present and future.

Most of the ideologues mentioned in this chapter have cut themselves off from the past, don't give a damn about the future, and care only about their present success.

What has this to do with business? Everything.

Gertrude Stein once explained her dislike for an American city: "There is no there there." It was merely a space-binding entity. Businesses as well as governments can suffer from this disease. Who is responsible? The business leaders who sincerely believe that "goodness has nothing to do with it," that short-term gains are all that matter. There are, of course, various degrees of moral obtuseness and moral "goodness." Only when we add the concept of time-binding to Kohlberg's moral stages can we evaluate how well we are really doing.

Stop and Go Ethics

In its ceaseless search for the utterly gross, the *New York Post* early in 1985 outdid itself: BOY SWALLOWS GAS, EXPLODES. Like the headline, many moral "truths" tell us what we should not do, but precious few go beyond "truth or consequences." As Thoreau says, being good is not enough. You must be good for something. Moral philosophers, relying on a priori reasoning, often deduce what is good or bad by relying on negation: a "logical" proposition formed by asserting the falsity of a given proposition.

What is logical to a philosopher or theologian cannot and should not intrude on the considerations of ulilitarian business people. Governments have shown that ideologues can become firmly entrenched in public affairs as well as private affairs, sometimes with disastrous results, but it is a luxury that business people can seldom afford. Utilitarianism fits in more comfortably with business affairs. In its broadest sense it holds that the determination of right conduct is the usefulness of its consequences. Thoreau and Korzybski would certainly concur.

The trouble with many of the moral "systems" mentioned in this book is not that they do not aim for moral "good" but that they are shortsighted. Most deal with *one* relationship in each game. No business person can hope to survive by always looking for the "one and only." Even the lottery offers better odds than that.

Korzybski underlines the perils of this course of action:

"Because we are human beings we are all of us interested in what we call progress—progress in law, in government, in jurisprudence, in ethics, in the natural sciences, in economics, in the fine arts, in the production and distribution of wealth, in all the affairs affecting the welfare of mankind. . . ."

He goes on to note that all of these "great matters" are interdependent and all must advance at the same pace in order to "maintain the integrity and continued prosperity . . . of our social life." In actuality, each advances at a different rate and obeys a different law of progress. As "the balance and equilibrium among the parts is disturbed, the strain gradually increases until a violent break ensues. . . ." The readjustment that follows "does indeed establish a kind of new equilibrium, but it is an equilibrium born of violence, and it is destined to be again disturbed periodically. . . ."

Why the different rates of progress? Korzybski attributes it to the simple arithmetical progress of the so-called "social" sciences and the geometrical progress of the "exact" sciences.

This brings into focus the "bottom line" of the Prisoner's Dilemma game as played at Harvard and in Axelrod's computer tournament. The awful truth is that no matter what arbitrary figure you assign to the rewards and punishments, your final score will indicate an arithmetical progression (or regression). Better to follow the advice of the Book of Genesis: "Be fruitful and multiply, and replenish the earth, and subdue it: and have dominion over the fish of the sea, and over the fowl of the air, and over every living thing that moveth upon the earth."

General Semantics and Ethics

Korzybski asks why the social sciences, including ethics, have lagged behind and gives his answer: "They have lagged behind, partly because they have been hampered by the traditions and the habits of a bygone world—they have looked backward instead of forward; they have lagged behind, partially because they have depended upon the barren methods of verbalistic philosophy—they have been metaphysical instead of scientific; they have lagged behind, partly because they have been often dominated by the lusts of cunning 'politicians' instead of being led by the wisdom of enlightened statesmen; they have lagged behind, partly because they have been predominately concerned to protect 'vested interests' upon which in the main they have depended for support; the *fundamental* cause, however, of their lagging behind is in the astonishing fact that, despite their being by their very nature most immediately concerned with the affairs of mankind, they have not discovered what Man really is but have from time immemorial falsely regarded human beings either as animals or else as combinations of animals and something supernatural."

Here again we can clearly identify the first five stages of moral reasoning as formulated by Kohlberg. The "special interests" that dominate the ethics of most people are the loyalties felt on each stage. The sixth stage is generally regarded as a combination of the animal and the supernatural. Such beings are seldom encountered outside of mythology and therefore provide a convenient excuse for non-achievers. Korzybski's concept of time-binding, however, makes that position untenable.

In "General Semantics and Human Values" (*General Semantics Bulletin*, Winter–Spring, 1952), Dr. J. S. A. Bois reports: "Our course has become a full program of study and application of 'G. S. Methods for Executives,' and it has been used in varying degrees by individuals or groups of executives. . . . They generally report that it makes them 'better men,' more willing to 'give and take,' etc. Some eventually discover 'that G. S. gives a scientific foundation to the Golden Rule,' some see in it a revised version of 'the Christian ideal of humility and charity.' But they fail to recognize in *Science and Sanity*, and most other books they read, an explicit rationale of what they experience."

Bois notes:

> Man interacts with chemicals, plants and animals, and he selects and binds in space-time the energies of all creation including his own and those of his fellow humans. Man moves back and forth in a four-dimensional world, being related and relating himself of his own initiative to those that went before him and to those that will follow him. This relatedness is "essential" to him, it is there for him to recognize; it is not added to an isolated existence that is his to share, or not to share at will. There is a form of "natural" energy specifically human, which operates according to the law of time-binding, and which, once discovered, makes possible developments that could not be achieved formerly.
>
> This view of the world and of man forces upon us ethical conclusions and duties. "On this inherently human level of interdependence, time-binding leads inevitably to feelings of responsibility, duty toward others and the future. . . ."

Henry IV and Rupert I

Henry IV of France is recognized in history as one of the most popular and able rulers of France. He fostered the development of commerce and industry and brought unprecedented prosperity to his country. He is also a striking example of the benefits of time-binding.

Brought up as a Calvinist, he fought against the Catholic League in the Wars of Religion as prince and later as king of Navarre. As heir presumptive to the throne of France he continued his war against the Catholics, won and was crowned king. Catholic opposition to his rule continued and finally in 1593 he embraced Catholicism and according to tradition said, "Paris is well worth a mass." In a lesser human being this might be regarded as a cynical solution but in Henry's case his recognition of the equal weight of past, present and future, brought peace and prosperity to a war-torn France. Besides, who could not help admiring an absolute monarch who said, "I want there to be no peasant in my realm so poor that he will not have a chicken in his pot every Sunday."

Rupert Murdoch, the press baron, on the other hand, in 1985 announced that he also was going to make a sacrifice to achieve his goal. Having turned two fine newspapers in Chicago and New York into schlock, he was willing to sell them because he wanted to build a television empire. (It's against the law to own a television station and a newspaper in the same city.) Like Henry, however, he faced another conflict of loyalties. He was an Australian citizen and only U. S. citizens can own a majority interest in U. S. television stations. His choice was simple: he would become a U. S. citizen.

Let us give him every benefit of the doubt. Was his stand morally "right"? Here's an editorial published in his *New York Post* (May 14, 1985):

Paul Thayer is an unusual criminal. He has been a decorated Navy flier, chairman of the U.S. Chamber of Commerce and Deputy Secretary of Defense. Last week he was sentenced to four years in the slammer.

Thayer's crime was that, while he was chairman and CEO of the LTV Corp., he passed on inside information to his broker about forthcoming corporate acquisitions. That netted his friends a stock market killing of $3 million. Then, under oath, Thayer lied about this illegal "insider trading."

So, Thayer was caught with his friends' hands in the till. He should be punished. But does he deserve a four-year jail sentence?

Several commentators not famous for their severity toward crime, including the editorial writers of the *New York Times* and the *Daily News*, argue indignantly that he does. Three broad justifications are advanced.

White collar crime, they say, is every bit as bad as street crime. It too hurts victims and inconveniences society. Now, some white collar crime does hurt its victims as much as a mugging—dumping toxic waste that poisons people, for instance.

What harm was done to Thayer's victims? Well, they sold their stock at a lower price than they would have done if they had been privy to his information. Some might have unloaded their stock anyway. The rest suffered the real harm of not making an unexpected capital gain. But does this compare with being beaten half-senseless by a gang?

As for inconvenience to society, when was the last time you were afraid to go out at night in case you were embezzled?

They argue, secondly, that muggers, rapists and vandals may not be deterred by jail, but that, to quote the *Daily News*, " . . . jail is the best—the only—deterrent for elegant, white-haired gentlemen in $800 suits."

This is nonsense on stilts. An apparently respectable businessman caught out in chicanery, like Thayer, is a ruined man. Being branded as a thief is a real punishment to him and so a real deterrent to other potential white collar thieves. But a mugger or a burglar is not ruined by being exposed as such. He does not lose his street reputation— possibly he enhances it.

Finally, it is said by the *Times* that "equal justice would be mocked if Thayer were given a lighter sentence than citizens less well placed." And so it would. But he is in fact being given a *heavier* sentence than others.

Thayer is a first offender with a hitherto unblemished reputation. A mugger in New York could plea-bargain his first offense—and with any luck his next ten—down to mere probation in an hour and still consider himself hard done by.

That's bad—and no sort of precedent for Thayer. He committed a crime and should suffer the proper punishment.

But the solemn crowing over his four-year sentence has nothing to do with justice. It is simply venting social revenge on people who have the temerity to wear $800 suits.

Test your moral I.Q. What moral lesson does this editorial teach? (Wearing a white collar while dumping "toxic waste that poisons people" is too obvious to count.)

CONCLUSION

Time-binding establishes priorities that make your contributions to the future morally good and good for something.

In America, some believe that Swift was wrong. White Americans won't eat any more inferior black children. They're "fed up" with that menu.

Defending the indefensible costs at least 10 times as much as the original moral offense.

Christ said: "Suffer the little children to come unto me, and forbid them not: for of such is the kingdom of God." The federal government edited it to conform to current "realities."

Time-binding provides a fourth dimension where moral reasoning can move freely to bring benefits to all of mankind. It eliminates the artificial boundary between "them" and "us" and permits us to cooperate so everyone can win.

CHAPTER

X

A Tale of Two Bishops

> There is a world of difference between "moral
> ideas"—ideas internalized so as to affect and im-
> prove conduct—and "ideas about morality"—the
> pieties we acknowledge verbally and then proceed
> to ignore. Talking about morality, honesty or kin-
> dliness in no way insures that people will act mor-
> ally, honestly or kindly. The job of the educator is
> to teach in such a way as to convert "ideas about
> morality" into "moral ideas."
>
> —CHARLES E. SILBERMAN,
> *Crisis in the Classroom*

THIS IS PRECISELY THE DIFFICULTY with TIT FOR TAT. In the either/or world of Game Theory, cooperation is "better" but defection is sometimes necessary to teach the value of long-term cooperation. If you are dealing with a person who always defects, according to the game rules, both of you will lose after the first move. If your opposer's and your strategy is TIT FOR TAT, but your opposer occasionally defects at random, the odds are that both of you will always also end up defecting. TIT FOR TAT "talks about morality" and can operate on any of the moral stages, but at the postconventional stages five and six it clearly is seen as manipulative and offensive to individuals with "moral ideas."

The columnist Beth Fallon took on this moral problem (New York *Daily News*, November 21, 1984) and suggested a "better," longer-lasting solution than TIT FOR TAT. Her target was Archbishop John J. O'Connor (Rear Admiral, USN, Ret.). During his first eight months in New York, the archbishop said that if politics is understood "as a people's ongoing attempt to set the standards by which they will be governed," then bishops cannot remain silent on such issues as the arms race, abortion and economic justice.

The recently installed archbishop, a few months before the 1984 presidential election, had exhorted Governor Mario Cuomo and Representative Geraldine A. Ferraro, both Catholics, to work for an end to legalized abortion. They argued that they could not translate their personal and religious antagonism to abortion into public policy because abortion had widespread public support and also that the Supreme Court had ruled that abortion was a Constitutional right. As a public official, Cuomo added, he had sworn to uphold the Constitution and could not violate that oath.

The archbishop was not pleased with their stand and hinted that Catholics should vote against "any" politician holding it.

Having criticized Democratic officeholders on the state and national levels, the archbishop then took on Mayor Ed Koch when Koch attempted to enforce an executive order barring discrimination against homosexuals in city-financed public service work. Both the New York diocese of the Roman Catholic Church and the Salvation Army refused to sign contracts with such a clause because of religious principles and won their case in court on a technicality. Both religious groups said that homosexuality was a sin in their eyes and could not be condoned. The Brooklyn diocese, however, had no such qualms about hiring "sinners." Even in Brooklyn, saints are in short supply.

Martin E. Marty, professor of the history of modern Christianity, has observed: "Those who speak in the name of God have the hardest time learning that politics is the art of compromise. Politics involves give-and-take: You win some, you lose some. The prophets of God who are too sure of themselves expect only to take, to win."

In his bouts with the mayor, the congresswoman and the governor, Archbishop O'Connor played to win against three consummate politicians. How did he do? Fallon's column gives his self-evaluation:

Archbishop John J. O'Connor talked about human potential yesterday to the Association for a Better New York. The most interesting human potential he talked about was his. "What would *you* do," he asked the assembled bankers, real-estate magnates, power brokers and government officials, "if you found yourself archbishop of New York?"

There was a sort of stunned silence in the room. "Within the responsibilities, what would you do? How would you marshal the resources? . . . I have been given the responsibility for the spiritual care of almost two million Catholics. Obviously, with it goes a responsibility to the common good.

"I don't know how to do it. . . . I don't know how to reach out and discover the best way to serve."

A power broker had a suggestion which he confided to Fallon: "Don't be an admiral in New York. I have known three admirals in my life. One was a banker after retirement. One was a businessman. And one is now an archbishop. They all loved to give orders. It's the Navy training. Nobody has so much power as a ship's captain and admirals get the habit even worse."

Commenting on the diversity of the audience—politicians, business leaders, and representatives of various religious groups—Fallon concluded her column with this advice:

With such disparity, New York most needs not an admiral, but a shepherd. "I know mine and mine know me," it says in the Christian gospels. But it also mentions others "not of this fold." And lost lambs, some people have complained then and since, got an inordinate amount of sympathy and attention. . . .

New York is full of lost lambs—rich, poor and in between. It is full of wolves, too. There is indeed more work for a shepherd than an admiral here. An archbishop who wears that humble hat is bound to be a success. No matter what color the hat is. [Fallon refers to the expected elevation of O'Connor to a cardinal, who wears a red hat, but still a shepherd's hat.]

One of the interesting factors in the dispute between Archbishop O'Connor and Governor Cuomo is that although both were Catholics and cooperated at the start, TIT FOR TAT did not seem to work for either of them. In September, 1984, Cuomo told an audience at the University of Notre Dame that he personally opposed abortion but did not favor seeking laws to restrict it. He said a sufficient consensus did not exist and that attempts to end it would be unworkable. He upheld the right of bishops to speak out on moral issues but said Catholics should refrain from trying to impose church doctrine on the general public and should teach by example rather than by seeking legal remedies.

In his reply, O'Connor stressed that the greatest public need faced by political figures was to "protect the rights of the unborn." He continued: "I recognize the dilemma confronted by some Catholics in political life. I cannot resolve that dilemma for them. As I see it, their disagreement, if they do disagree, is not simply with me; it is with the teaching of the Catholic Church."

TIT FOR TAT did not work for either man on the personal level because, however much they may have initially desired to cooperate, they soon found themselves always defecting, the archbishop with his stage-four certainty that a law would "solve" a complex social problem, and the governor with his stage-five certainty that arbitrary laws, however "good" or "bad" their intention, could not solve anything.

Within the context of the game theory, both men "lost" on the personal level but their losses were minimized. At the same time, on their separate levels of moral reasoning, both "won" by cooperating with many of their followers. For a politician—or a bishop—that is what counts. Making converts to their side counts for even more.

Interestingly, Ferraro was the only one to lose on both the personal and moral level. On the personal level, both she and the archbishop "lost," just as he and Cuomo had.

Axelrod says: "Cooperation Theory has implications for individual choice as well as for the design of institutions. Speaking personally, one of my biggest surprises in working on this project has been the value of provocability. I came to this project believing one should be slow to anger. The results of the Computer Tournament for the Prisoner's Dilemma demonstrate that it is actually better to respond quickly to a provocation. It turns out that if one waits to respond to uncalled-for defections, there is a risk of sending the wrong signal."

Ferraro, in her debate with Vice President Bush, however, was pressured into attempting to bridge the gap between Church and State by cooperating rather than defecting. She said [cooperating as a Catholic] that if she were faced with a choice between continuing to hold office and committing an immoral act she would resign. Many regarded this as a sign of weakness and as "unpresidential." It certainly was atypical of the view of most political leaders. Very few would agree with Henry Clay's "I would rather be right than be President." In a democracy, anyone so certain of his rectitude does not deserve to be in that high office. There is more to morality than any single issue.

That is why TIT FOR TAT is effective on the first four stages of moral reasoning and manipulative in forcing actions and reactions on stages five and six. As Axelrod says, "It is actually better to respond quickly to provocation." (This, of course, assumes that the opposers are equals and operating on the same moral level.)

Can we recognize what constitutes provocation and what is the "appropriate" response?

On stage one, provocation is annoying or angering an authority figure. The "appropriate" response is to cast the culprit into the outer darkness.

On stage two, the provocation is not to reciprocate, or to compel. The "appropriate" response is to defect. If a computer can be made to operate on a moral level, this is it.

On stage three, provocation and the "appropriate" response are whatever the group says they are.

On stage four, provocation is "crime" and the appropriate response is "punishment."

On stage five, defection is treated as an aberration not requiring punishment but distraction. TIT FOR TAT would be regarded as manipulation because "all" the defector wants is his share of the pie. Give it to him! Keep him in the fold!

On stage six, the "defection" of others is irrelevant. The moral ideas by which you live are all-important. You do not rely on laws to enforce your moral ideas. Compulsion and defection do not rescue "lost sheep," they drive them further into the wilderness. The Book of Isaiah describes a way to implant moral ideas: "He shall feed his flock like a shepherd: he shall gather the lambs with his arm, and carry them in his bosom, and shall gently lead those that are with young."

Desmond Tutu, Anglican bishop of Johannesburg, South Africa, and winner of the 1984 Nobel Peace Prize, has exhibited that kind of leadership in his unrelenting battle against apartheid. In a speech in New York City (December 3, 1983) he attacked the Reagan administration's policy of "constructive engagement"—a TIT FOR

TAT strategy that maintained relations with South Africa but avoided outspoken criticism in the hope of winning reform.

"Where's the anger?" the bishop asked. "Constructive engagement has given a bad name to democracy. Constructive engagement is an abomination, an unmitigated disaster." Yet he began his speech with a joke that implanted his moral ideas in the audience's mind better than any order or harsh criticism could have done:

"When the missionaries first came to Africa, they had the Bible and we had the land. They said, 'Let us pray.' We closed our eyes. When we opened them, the tables had been turned. We had the Bible and they had the land."

This gentle leadership produced waves of laughter but also taught a lesson. As Paul Moore, the Episcopal bishop of New York, said: "A hero. But a disarming kind of hero." No lost lambs here.

CONCLUSION

Moral certainty—used as a club—encourages defection. Used as a shepherd's crook, it can induce cooperation. The first makes TIT FOR TAT a manipulative strategy that produces a "winner" and a "loser." The second permits cooperation to flourish for the good of all society.

CHAPTER
XI

The Self-Made Man

ONE OF THE MOST CURIOUS BY-PRODUCTS of social Darwinism is the so-called self-made man. To the degree that hard work has brought material rewards, there is much to admire and perhaps envy in such a person. When he goes beyond the average, surpasses or excels others in exploiting his talents, outachieves, outperforms, outproduces—no rational person can begrudge him his rewards. When, however, he outintrigues, outmanipulates and outpromises, people at the fifth or sixth stage of moral reasoning are less likely to cooperate, more likely to defect. After all, "He started it." Since he is "self-made," he owes nothing to anyone but himself. He always plays a zero-sum game (described in the Game Theory matrix) and demands to be the winner.

If, by chance, you have not encountered such a person this letter in the *Washington Post* (December 13, 1984) written by Lou Gehrig Burnett will prove instructive:

When I read Kevin R. Hopkins' article "The Tax Plan Goes Easy on the Family—Finally," I felt it was time to vent my feelings—finally—as a single taxpayer.

The liberal "bleeding hearts" have been successful in fostering an attitude in this country that if someone works hard and does well, he or she should give up most of it to help those who won't help themselves.

I don't want to. After working my way—day and night—through six years of college, I, as a single taxpayer, do not want to give my earnings to the government to spend on giveaway programs and on individuals who rely on the government to take care of them from cradle to grave.

Why should I subsidize married couples who have babies? If they can't afford the kids, they shouldn't have them. And if they want to go to college, let them work their way through instead of depending on ol' overburdened Uncle Sam. And why should I subsidize a single parent because he or she could not make a relationship work?

I'm tired of paying more for things, such as schools, that I don't use. Why not tax people according to the services they use? For example, the more kids they have, the more taxes they pay.

Let's stop the juggernaut toward a classless society, and let the family unit assume some of the responsibility for its members for a change.

There, I've said it.

Yes, indeed you have, Lou Gehrig Burnett. But, you, the reader, may ask, is it morally "right" or "wrong"? For the business person, that may be hard to answer. Kohlberg's stages are of little help. Obviously Burnett alone has chosen the moral principles by which he lives and is ready to act alone, if need be, to fulfill what he believes in. No matter how much the "bleeding hearts" may protest, he *seems* to be firmly at stage six.

A "few simple rules" by Laura L. Nash reveal no moral flaw. TIT FOR TAT is exactly what is demanded. He has paid enough. Now it's someone else's turn. We do not even know if Thoreau's test, "Be not simply good; be good for something," is applicable. We do not know the source of the wealth that so entices the tax collector. Korzybski, alone among the moralists we have considered, provides a plausible theory: He may be among "those whose profession is to fight for the division of things produced by nature or by other human beings."

Korzybski's *Manhood of Humanity*, which has been quoted throughout this book, sheds further light on social Darwinism and its bizarre offspring, the self-made man. The book lists three cardinal classes of life:

[T]hough minerals have various activities, they are not "living." The plants have a very definite and well-known function—the transformation of solar energy into organic chemical energy. They are a class of life which appropriates one kind of energy, converts it into another kind and stores it up; in that sense they are a kind of storage battery for the solar energy; and so I define THE PLANTS AS THE CHEMISTRY-BINDING class of life.

The animals use the highly dynamic products of the *chemistry-binding* class—the plants—as food and those products—the results of plant-transformation—undergo in animals a further transformation into yet higher forms; and the animals are correspondingly a more dynamic class of life; their energy is kinetic; they have a remarkable freedom and power which the plants do not possess—I mean the freedom and faculty to move about in space; and so I define ANIMALS AS THE SPACE-BINDING CLASS OF LIFE.

Korzybski then defines the time-binding class as quoted in Chapter III, concluding with this:

These definitions of the cardinal classes of life are, it will be noted, obtained from direct observation; they are so simple and so important that I cannot over-emphasize the necessity of grasping them and most especially the definition of Man. For these simple definitions and especially that of Humanity will profoundly transform the whole conception of human life in every field of interest and activity; and, what is more important than all, the definition of Man will give us a starting point for discovering the *natural* laws of human nature—of the human class of life. The definitions of the classes of life represent the different classes as distinct in respect to dimensionality; and this is extremely important for no measure or rule of one class can be applied to the other, *without making grave mistakes.* For example, to treat a human being as an animal—as a mere space-binder—because humans have certain animal propensities, is an error of the same type and grossness as to treat a cube as a surface because it has surface properties. It is absolutely essential to grasp that fact if we are ever to have a science of human nature.

How does Burnett stack up against this assessment? Not well. He regards himself as a mere space-binder. The beginning of his life is the "beginning" of humanity. Its end is "oblivion" for all. Nothing of him remains in humanity's memory. Even his space has been redistributed by other self-made men.

Ann Crittenden in "The Age of 'Me-First Management' " (*New York Times*, August 19, 1984) is one of many who find that "America's corporate chiefs are losing sight of moral standards in the new frenzy to get rich":

> It doesn't take a revolutionary to figure out that something is amiss in American business today; that a 'me-first, grab-what-you-can' extravagance increasingly appears to be cropping up among the nation's top executives. It shows itself in the disproportionate salaries and bonuses paid to so many corporate chiefs; in the unseemly scrambling over the assets of great corporations; in the multimillion-dollar severance payments awarded even to C.E.O.'s who fail and drive their companies into the ground.

Seymour Melman, professor of industrial engineering at Columbia University, has written a fascinating book, *Profits Without Production* (New York: Alfred A. Knopf, 1983), which details the tragic (and immoral) deterioration of our space-binding capabilities and our failure to apply Korzybski's "human engineering" to today's weighty problems. As an engineer, Melman deplores a "generation of managers . . . trained by our business school to make money, not goods." American managers were once the world's best organizers of industrial work. A social contract was in effect: In return for its decision-making power and wealth, management was expected by society to invest in and efficiently operate the means of production.

> In the last 25 years, management's social contract with workers and the community has been broken as managers have turned from making goods to making money by means other than production. The result of this transformation in management's professional imperatives is vis-

ible in the dissolution of production competence in once-great industries.

Is this immoral or unethical? Korzybski would emphatically say "Yes".

It is fatal to apply the "survival of the fittest" theory in the same sense to two radically different classes of life. The "survival of the fittest" for animals—for *space*-binders—is survival *in space*, which means fighting and other brutal forms of struggle; on the other hand, "survival of the fittest" for human beings *as such*—that is, for *time-binders*—is survival *in time*, which means intellectual or spiritual competition, struggle for excellence, for making the *best* survive. The fittest-in-time—those who make the best survive—are those who do the most in producing values for all mankind including *posterity*. This is the scientific base for natural ethics, and ethics from which there can be no side-stepping, or escape.

Here we have confirmation, out of all the systems that have been discussed, that Lou Gehrig Burnett and other "self-made men" like him do not measure up ethically because they do not admit the debt they owe to the past and their obligation to posterity. They have staked out the space they will occupy and will defend it tooth and claw. Even their material success is suspect. As Albert Einstein once said, "What a person thinks on his own without being stimulated by the thoughts and experiences of other people is even in the best case rather petty and monotonous."

Korzybski also expands on the Lord High Executioner's "little list" of society offenders who might well be underground and "who never would be missed":

Such are the children of folly: (1) Drifting fools—ignorers of the past—disregarders of race experience—thoughtless floaters on the shifting currents of human affairs; (2) Static fools—idealizers of the past—complacent lovers of the present—enemies of change—fearful of the future; (3) Dynamic fools—scorners of the past—haters of the present—destroyers of the work of the dead—most *modest* of fools, each of them saying: "What ought to be begins with *Me;* I will make the world a paradise; but my genius must be free; now it is hampered by the existing 'order'—the bungling work of the past; I will destroy it; I will start with chaos; we need light—the Sun casts shadows—I will begin by blotting out the Sun; then the world will be full of glory—the light of my genius."

Clearly, the so-called "self-made men" are of the first category—the drifting fools. The second category is also in plentiful supply. For example, this letter appeared in the *New York Times*, January 2, 1985:

> To the Editor:
>
> A group of Roman Catholic nuns says the Vatican has imperiled the right of Catholics to free speech. The Vatican has done nothing of the kind.
>
> The Vatican merely defends the ancient "magisterium"—the authority to teach true doctrine—in the matter of faith and morals, and to claim to speak for the church when one supports opinions contrary to the magisterium is as ludicrous as a schoolmaster claiming to teach English when in fact he lectures on mathematics. Believing Catholics hold themselves bound to a revealed religion, not to speculation of any stray discussion group.
>
> There have been others besides these nuns who have departed from the discipline of Rome while maintaining a nostalgic attachment to the notion of Catholicity: they are known as Protestants.

Yes, indeed, Dennis Crowley, they are, and a giant of the Protestant Reformation, Martin Luther, on the 500th anniversary of his birth in 1983, was honored by Pope John Paul II, the first pope ever to attend a Lutheran Church service. Although a conservative in the best sense of the word, the Pope expressed, as Crowley would say, a certain "nostalgic attachment" to the teachings of an ex-priest who married a nun, sired six children and was excommunicated by the church because he could not tolerate what he considered to be its corruption. His famous statement, at the Diet of Worms, "Here I stand, I cannot do otherwise," is a sterling example of stage-six moral reasoning. It also ushered in the religious wars that plagued Europe for hundreds of years.

Dynamic fools are in such great supply that everyone has his own "Great Satan" to serve as a model. But what of the "fittest-in-time—

those who make the best survive, who do the most in producing values for all mankind including posterity?"

One of my favorite moral statements from the past is Jefferson's Declaration of Independence. Another is advice from an aged follower of St. Francis of Assisi, quoted in *Saint Francis* by Leonardo Boff (New York: Crossroads, 1984):

> If you feel the call of the Spirit, then be holy with all your soul, with all your heart, and with all your strength.
>
> If, however, because of human weakness you cannot be holy, then be perfect with all your soul, with all your heart, and with all your strength.
>
> But, if you cannot be perfect because of vanity in your life, then be good with all your soul, with all your heart, and with all your strength.
>
> Yet, if you cannot be good because of the trickery of the Evil One, then be wise with all your soul, with all your heart, and with all your strength.
>
> If, in the end, you can be neither holy, nor perfect, nor good, nor wise because of the weight of your sins, then carry this weight before God and surrender your life to His divine mercy.
>
> If you do this, without bitterness, with all humility, and with a joyous spirit due to the tenderness of God Who loves the sinful and ungrateful, then you will begin to feel what it is to be wise, you will learn what it is to be good, you will slowly aspire to be perfect and finally, you will long to be holy.

These words inspired by the teachings of St. Francis who lived 800 years ago, transcend Kohlberg's six stages. They view life as a process and point out one way of negotiating yourself intellectually or spiritually to a position where you can indeed produce values for all mankind.

CONCLUSION

"Survival of the fittest" insures the well-being of the biggest rat in the pack, but goodness has nothing to do with it.

To be good for something, you must start somewhere. The concept of time-binding frees you from self-imposed limitations and permits you to rise to your highest level of moral competency.

If you can see the world as T. S. Eliot saw it:

> Time present and time past
> Are both perhaps present in time future,
> And time future contained in time past

perhaps you can rise above mere competency and see the world as William Blake did:

> To see a world in a grain of sand,
> And a heaven in a wild flower
> Hold infinity in the palm of your hand
> And eternity in an hour.

Appendix A

ONE SUCH GAME THEORY matrix, as reported by Solman and Friedman, was this:

		B	
		B1	B2
A	A1	($5,$5)	(−$5,$10)
	A2	($10,−$5)	(−$2,−$2)

In this game, two players play only once and the goal is to do as well as possible. If the A player chose strategy A1, and the B player chose B1, both would win $5. If the A player chose A1, and the B player, B2, A would lose $5 and B would gain $10. The results would be reversed if A played A2 and B played B1. However, if they played A2 and B2, both would lose $2. The course instructor commented to two students who played A2, B2, "You have been logical, but you have lost. That is the most interesting lesson of this game: Rational behavior ends up hurting both players."

Six players in the class played strategy one. Four of them "lost" badly. The other two playing "against" each other "won" $5 each. For this transgression against stage-two morality, whose aim is to maximize pleasure and minimize pain, the instructor offered this comment. "So you trusted each other, because the stakes of the game were small and the stakes of your friendship were higher. The real payoffs, for you, weren't in the matrix. What would you have done if the numbers were in the thousands of dollars and the game was for real?"

Perhaps their nonverbal communication hinted at what they said after class: That they would have done the same, no matter what the stakes. In any event, the instructor dismissed their aberration as the exception that proves the rule.

"When people play this game in the laboratory, and it's a one-shot thing, then everybody chooses strategy two, once they understand what's going on. Of course, you have to make sure that what counts is the payoffs, and there's not some consideration of friendship or something else, because then the numbers won't represent the real payoffs to the players. . . ."

After this unedifying prologue, the instructor got down to the nitty-gritty of managerial gamesmanship. He stated that no matter how many times you repeat the game, "if you were logical to an extreme," you would repeat strategy two every time, even if the game is played 20 times. The reason? "You know that on the last round you're going to attack, the other guy knows that too, so there is no goodwill to establish on the nineteenth move . . . so you do it on the eighteenth move. . . . Logic, then, dictates that you should do it on the first move. The other will follow, so you both will lose.

"On the other hand, if you choose strategy two too late, then the other guy will very probably attack before you, so on that one move you will be socked. You have to try to anticipate and attack just one move before the other guy would"—so *he* would "get socked."

Appendix B

	Player B	
	C Cooperation	D Defection
Player A C Cooperation	R = 3 Reward for mutual cooperation	S = 0 Sucker's payoff
D Defection	T = 5 Temptation to defect	P = 1 Punishment for mutual defection

Fig. 1. The Prisoner's Dilemma game. *The payoff to player A is* shown with illustrative numerical values. The game is defined by $T > R > P > S$ and $R > (S + T) \div 2$.

In this "simple" game, each player is confronted with an either/or choice: either cooperate or defect. The payoff, however, is determined by the choices of *both* parties. If both cooperate they are rewarded equally but not as much as one would be if he defected and the other cooperated. This is the supreme lesson taught at Harvard. The "sucker" (or cooperator) gets nothing if the other player defects. The defector wins big.

Axelrod views this matter dispassionately:

> If the other player cooperates, there is a choice between cooperation which yields R . . . or defection which yields T . . . By assumption, T>R so that it pays to defect if the other player cooperates. On the other hand, if the other player defects, there is a choice between co-operation, which yields S . . . or defection, which yields P . . . by assumption P>S, so it pays to defect if the other player defects. Thus, no matter what the other player does, it pays to defect. But, if both defect, both get P rather than the larger value of R that they both could have gotten had both cooperated. Hence the dilemma.

P.D.G.